An American Traveler

AN AMERICAN TRAVELER

True Tales of Adventure, Travel, and Sport

Randy Wayne White

THE LYONS PRESS

GUILFORD, CONNECTICUT

AN IMPRINT OF THE GLOBE PEQUOT PRESS

The Lyons Press is an imprint of The Globe Pequot Press.

All of these stories, in shorter or edited form, appeared in *Outside* magazine between the years 1995 and 1997.

Printed in the United States of America

10 9 8 7 6 5 4 3 2 1

Designed by Stephanie Doyle

ISBN 1-59228-033-1

Library of Congress Cataloging-in-Publication Data

White, Randy Wayne.
  An American traveler : true tales of adventure, travel, and sports / Randy Wayne White.
      p. cm.
  ISBN 1-59228-033-1 (hc : alk. paper)
  1. White, Randy Wayne—Travel. 2. Voyages and travels. I. Title.
  G465.W49 2003
  910.4—dc22
                                          2003018052

Years ago, when I was a fishing guide on Sanibel Island, Florida, *Outside* magazine's editors and contributors not only encouraged me to write, they elevated my work by example. Their impact on my life has been immense. This book is dedicated to them, with affection and gratitude. A few to whom I'd like to give special thanks are Terry McDonell, John Rasmus, Mark Bryant, Larry Burke, Donovan Webster, Hampton Sides, Laura Hohnhold, Craig Vetter, Tim Cahill, David Quammen, Jon Krakauer, Bob Shacochis, and Geoffrey Norman.

ACKNOWLEDGMENT

———————

A CENTURY FROM NOW, and more, publisher and sportsman Tony Lyons will still be admired for his vision as the literary conservator of all things outdoors. It is thanks only to him that some writers, and their work—otherwise lost during this or the previous century—may still be around as well.

AUTHOR'S NOTE

EVEN THOUGH SPORTING EVENTS AGE QUICKLY, I've included my account of New Zealand's successful bid to win the '95 America's Cup ("No More Curse of the Sheepherders") as a tribute to the late Sir. Peter Blake.

I've had a soft spot for Kiwi Cup campaigns that dates back to 1987, Fremantle, Australia. When the Dennis Connor syndicate refused to allow me into their compound, saying I wasn't qualified (I wasn't), I thought I was screwed, along with my piece for Outside. The sympathetic New Zealanders, however, came to the rescue. They not only invited me into their area, they took me into their house (Kasa Kiwi), to their parties, onto their boats, then secretly cancelled my flight back to the States so I could stay and have more fun.

It was a different Kiwi team that won the '95 Cup, but the kindness and class of the New Zealanders was unchanged. Peter

Blake illustrated professionalism, and looked like Viking royalty, but was also one of the nicest, most decent guys you could meet. When I told him a pal of mine, manager of a major league baseball team, was on a losing streak, he gave me a pair of his "lucky" red sox to send him. When Black Magic won the final race, I suspect it was also Peter who made certain I was among the first Americans shepherded into the celebration.

On a December night, 2001, while on an Amazon cruise to raise environmental awareness, Blake's boat was boarded by nine masked thugs who called themselves "The River Rats." The Rats thought the lone sailor who confronted them would behave like a typical frightened tourist. They'd never met a great man before.

One of the last things Blake wrote in his journal that Wednesday, Dec. 5, was: "Dusk has turned the surface of the river into a greasy grey, with the sky quickly darkening after the sun's orange and golds have gone . . . .

"Again, I raise the question: why are we here? Our aim is to begin to understand the reasons why we must all start appreciating what we have before it is too late. We want to restart people caring for the environment as it must be cared for. We want to make a difference."

Sir Peter Blake did.

—RWW

CONTENTS

INTRODUCTION

———— •·•·• ————

I BELIEVE THAT WHERE I WORK becomes a part of what I write. A good writing space infuses subtleties of tone, sentence rhythms, plus shadings of color to a region I'm describing, even though the region may be an ocean away from my desk.

Since you're contemplating reading this collection of stories about unusual places, odd subjects, all of which have been flavored by the spot where they were created, it's a phenomenon that we should explore.

A bad writing space lacks energy. It seems fluorescent even when it doesn't have fluorescent lighting. A bad place isolates, but without the inspiring qualities of solitude.

I've gotten fussy about where I work. I have some favorites, and keep going back, especially when on deadline, finishing a book. There's the walled garden in the Hotel Santa Clara, Cartagena, Colombia, where the staff has fresh grapefruit juice waiting on my table each morning. On Useppa Island, one of Florida's oldest tarpon fishing resorts, there's an antiquated trophy room that smells of pine and overlooks the croquet court. In Key West, I like Old Cypress House, writing beneath ceiling fans near the pool, eager to get my work done and start enjoying the great happy hour spread that Dave, the manager, lays out.

Why some places are good to write and others bad I can't say. It seems to have more to do with alchemy than chemistry, so it'll probably remain a mystery, which is fine by me.

There are some necessities, however, that all good places share. I want a table or desk that isn't tippy. I want a comfortable chair. There can be noise, but it can't be the kind of noise that pauses unexpectedly so that I pause, too, waiting for the damn thing to start or stop again. I prefer simplicity to extravagance, and a place outside rather than inside.

A good example is my office. It's nicely appointed with executive furniture, bookshelves, electronic gadgets, computer, a wrap-around desk and an expensive executive's chair.

I almost never write there.

Instead, I work outside on the porch. I sit in a plastic chair. I type at a wooden table.

The porch is my favorite place in the world to work. Because most of these stories were composed there, I'd like you to be able to picture it so that you'll recognize the porch's influence when you read about white sharks in South Africa, playing baseball in Cuba, jogging among Mayan ruins, or the internal explorations dealing with fear or middle age.

The infusion is subtle, but the influence of my writing-place can be found in sentence rhythms, tone, and shadings of color, light, and style.

In our culture, the porch was once a powerful stage. I grew up listening to stories told on darkening porches, absorbing family history near Pee Dee River in Richmond County, North Carolina, and in small Ohio towns. I can think of no gathering place more beloved, or that better symbolizes rural, middle-class Americans.

Well-traveled or not, writing on a porch fits comfortably with what I am and will always be.

HOUSE ON A MOUND

—••—

DURING WORKING HOURS, the place I work is private, solitary. There's a sign out front telling potential visitors that it is so. Because I'm a sociable person, though, when I'm finished, the isolation changes with a kind of abrupt flair, like a curtain going up.

People love to visit, which is understandable. Their postcard ideal of old Florida may be the view from the west side of the porch, which looks out through coconut palms onto Pine Island Sound. It's a favorite spot to host strangers and roustabout friends, particularly around sunset, which is when I serve interesting combinations of cheese and home-grown chili peppers, hot sauces, and chutneys.

When I travel, I collect recipes to test and chili seeds to plant. So, just as the porch flavors my perception of travel, so do my travels spice up the porch.

Beer's kept in the back 'fridge. Foot traffic there is brisk.

I love my porch, and it's the image that comes to mind when I hear the word "home." There are reasons: It's plenty wide, wraps around three sides of the house, and is comfortably furnished. It has an outdoor shower, a hot tub, a hammock, a bed, and a mature avocado tree growing up through the roof, so it's a little like living in a tree house.

On windy nights, when the tree is fruiting, avocadoes sound like gunfire when they hit the tin roof—which once got a memorable reaction from a pal who feared his ex-wife was trying to have him killed.

On the porch's walls, I've nailed mementos at eye-level so I can look at them when I want, and take pleasure. There is the brass plaque stolen by friends from the wall outside Manuel Noriega's house during the invasion of Panama, and there's the sign from a Nicaraguan Embassy stolen by me. There are maps and charts from past trips. There are sharks jaws and tarpon scales, and oil lamps filled and ready, anticipating power outages caused by storms that come blowing in across the Gulf.

On the south wall is a neon beer sign that I light for friends to see when I am done working for the day. On the west wall is the sign that used to hang at Tarpon Bay Marina on Sanibel during the thirteen years I was a fishing guide:

CAPT. RANDY WHITE/LIGHT TACKLE TARPON/SHARK TAGGING/CABBAGE KEY DINNER TRIPS

The sign is there for me to see, and to remind me that our lives can take strange twists and interesting turns.

It is impossible to imagine my porch, or the way that it has influenced this book, unless you know a little something about where I live and about the people who were here before me. I live on an island in Cracker house built in the 1920s, painted yellow, with, as I mentioned, a tin roof. The house sits on the remains of a shell mound, or maybe a shell pyramid, that was inhabited for more than a thousand years by the indigenous people of this coast, the Calusa.

You will read a lot more about the Calusa in the first piece, "The Gold Medallion."

I like the fact that, when I rake the black soil in my chili garden, I find chunks of pottery—remnants of bowls used to feed fishermen who walked this mound centuries before me. I also treasure the knowledge that, among the Calusa were story tellers, and from this small place I continue to tell stories. There is a metaphorical linkage across ten centuries—a connection of which I am a part.

The stories inside, many of them touched by this place, are part of that linkage, too.

True, the linkage may be fanciful, but stand on this mound on the dark of the moon, in a wind that blows fresh out of Cuba, and the possibility of linkage will gain credence. Five hundred generations of sea people stood at this precise spatial intersection, feeling the same ocean wind.

That kind of power, it's hard to keep out of the story, no matter what you're writing about.

For instance, from the little wooden table where I've been typing, I can look out and rest my eyes upon a scene that is as common now as it was three hundred years ago: the bay is animated before me, iridescent in a wind that smells of rain. In the storm light, coconut palms leaning in strands are isolated by their height, top-heavy with fronds as dense as macaw feathers. The trees appear fragile and singular, gold on green, as if bent by a hurricane wind, then marooned in stillness.

There is scent, mood, and colors enough for a pallet. I might be in Central America. I might be revisiting South Africa.

This porch is a good place to write. For someone who has never traveled so far that he was able to leave his home behind, this porch is also good place to return.

—Randy Wayne White

AN AMERICAN TRAVELER

THE GOLD MEDALLION

———·•·•·———

THERE WAS A LIGHTNING STORM a few nights ago that knocked out all the power on the small island where I live. You have to know the circumstances to understand why it brought to mind a lost civilization, a ceremonial gold medallion, and the teenage boy who died shortly after pulling it from the Florida soil.

I was a couple of miles offshore at the time, heading back from a neighboring island in my flats skiff when—zap!—all lights vanished. The abruptness of it was disorienting. Those of us who live in solitary places think we know darkness. What we know is a diaphanous gray. When that grayness is extinguished unexpectedly, it's a little like standing on the lip of an abyss.

I backed the throttle, killed the engine, and waited. The rain hadn't reached me yet, but the wind was fierce. A Halloween moon rose above a tower of cumulus clouds. My island had taken on a strange new look. It was no longer a place of tin-roofed houses built upon Indian shell mounds. Tonight, it was a black mass elevated over the water, a dinosaur-shape afloat.

I stood at the boat's wheel, feeling the wind, and thought: This is the way it was when the Calusa were here.

At the time of Spanish contact in the sixteenth century, Florida's west coast was dominated by Calusa fishermen, hunters, and gatherers. Theirs was a sophisticated society. They were building and living on elaborate shell pyramids by the time of the Roman Empire, and their civilization lasted two hundred years after the arrival of the Spanish. In terms of human chronology, the high-rise hotels of Sarasota and the modern condominiums of Sanibel and Captiva Islands are but a few pale seconds in a long calendar day.

Although my own house happens to be built atop an Indian mound, I'm not a fanciful person. I've never seen Calusa ghosts. I've never communicated with the spirits of people who lived and worshiped and died right on the hillsides I now tend with a Sarlo lawn mower.

But when my island went black, it was easy for me to imagine the way it had been: temple mounds and sweeping plazas, networks of holding ponds for fish, priests presiding over human sacrifices, hand-dredged canals that led to the sea. And for just a moment, I could see a certain gold medallion, dangling from the neck of the son of a Calusa king as he walked among the thatch-roofed huts of his village. It might have been 1996, or it might have been a thousand years ago. Cut the electricity and the eyes are quick to readjust to primal light.

As I told Dr. William Marquardt, curator in archaeology of the Florida Museum of Natural History in Gainesville, "Considering all that's happened before and all that's happened since, you have to agree that the tale of the Calusa medallion sounds a little like a Stephen King novel."

Like most archaeologists, Marquardt is a pragmatist by training and a diplomat by necessity. "It's certainly alarming," he said. But it was clear from his unequivocal tone that as far as he was concerned, the story of the gold medallion had nothing to do with ghosts or the supernatural or, as some have said, the curse of a once-proud Native American tribe that was wiped out by European diseases, warfare, and slavery.

We were off the coast in my skiff, making a tour of the Calusa mounds. It was a few weeks after the lightning storm that had zapped all the power from my island. The west coast of Florida was once again tropic-bright, vacation-friendly.

"The remarkable thing about the Calusa," Marquardt told me, "is that although there's no uncontested evidence of horticulture, they still managed to create a culturally complex society. They built permanent towns. They developed elaborate art, a sophisticated religion, a formidable military, and a political system that relied on tribute sent by various chiefs under Calusa control. Unfortunately for us, that tribute sometimes included a tiny bit of gold and silver, probably taken from Spanish shipwrecks."

Unfortunate for archaeologists. And unfortunate for anyone who's interested in the pre-Columbian history of Florida.

This was our second day in the boat, yet we had visited only a few of the dozens of major habitation sites that range from Charlotte Harbor, about thirty-five miles north of Fort Myers, all the way down to Everglades National Park. Access to these islands isn't easy. To tourists charmed by Disney World and Florida's innumerable roadside attractions, the sites would be indistinguishable and, furthermore, unappealing: just a hedge of dense mangrove spreading out beneath a canopy of gumbo limbo trees. Most of the ruins were reachable only by shallow-draft boat.

At each site, Marquardt and I bushwhacked through monkey-bar prop roots and then made our way into the island's interior. We swatted sand flies and mosquitoes, ducked spider webs, dodged bayonet plants and prickly pear cacti. The vegetation of Florida soon strangles anything that doesn't move. Leave a plot of ground untended for a year and it will become jungle; most of these islands have been uninhabited for more than a century.

At one point, while picking a cactus spine out of my hand, I said to Marquardt, "You really enjoy busting your butt to get to these places?"

Marquardt, who looks like one might expect an archaeologist to look—eyeglasses, backpacker clothing, and a sparse beard—is a precise and methodical man. He's a gourmet cook and a musician. His interests are wide-ranging, but his professional focus is laser-like: He's hell-bent on protecting these ancient mounds and establishing a research center to study the Calusa. "Sure," he said. "It's a lot better than being in an office." Then he waved at the haze of gnats orbiting his face. "But I could do without these damn bugs. People are still arguing about how the Indians endured them."

How the Calusa endured is puzzling enough, but how they managed to prevail is truly mind-boggling. It's a stunning thing to hack your way through the jungle and come upon a man-made hill, thirty-eight feet high, covered with whelk shells the size of footballs. In the context of the mangrove littoral of west Florida, a thirty-eight-foot mound might as well be a mountain. The Calusa workers piled on the shells and shaped the contours, basketful after woven basketful. Like developers in modern times, these people erected their civilization upon the swamp.

"That's why it's so sad what's happened to the mounds," Marquardt said. During the early and mid-1900s, he explained, road builders used many mounds as fill. Many others have been destroyed by developers operating under Florida's modern economic ethic: The old girl's dying anyway, so go ahead and bite off a chunk.

But what really angered Marquardt was this: At nearly every site, cut deeply into each mound, one can find a multitude of holes, some of them the size of bomb craters. "Treasure hunters," Marquardt said. "Archaeologists all over the world have to contend with them. The thing is—Marquardt had to smile in frustration when he said this—"there's nothing here for them to find, unless they're looking for old shells. Nothing they could sell. It's unusual to find even a single large pottery shard. They didn't have stone, and the little bit of metal they had came from the Spaniards."

So what are they looking for?

"They're looking for treasure buried by a pirate named José Gaspar," Marquardt said. "And they're looking for metal ceremonial ornaments that are extremely rare and are unlikely to be in a shell mound anyway—like the one the little boy found near here."

In 1969, on an island off Florida's west coast, a fourteen-year-old boy named Rommie David Taylor and his younger brother were sifting for Indian artifacts when they unearthed a few human bones, a few Spanish chevron beads, and then a small, oddly designed pendant made of sheet gold.

It was sixty-four millimeters long and thirty-three millimeters wide, and weighed a little less than an ounce. On the medallion's face, concentric circles had been etched upon a cross. There were three bisecting lines, a pair of teardrop shapes, and a series of half-rectangles nested like doors within doors. On the medallion's back were several crescent-moon shapes, one above the other.

What was the medallion's significance to the Calusa culture? No one knew for sure, but according to early Spanish missionaries, the sons of Calusa kings wore a certain gold ornament on their foreheads as an emblem of rank. Perhaps, archaeologists surmised, the boy had stumbled upon one of these royal insignia.

David Taylor was blessed with a finely tuned radar for buried relics. As his mother, Lorraine, recalled, "David was far more interested in archaeology than, say, baseball. He read everything he could about the history of the Calusa, and he liked to hunt for artifacts. It was uncanny the way he could find things. Like the gold medallion—he was digging in a place that no one would think to look."

It's still not known for certain exactly where the boy was digging, but Marquardt believes that he had stumbled upon a burial ground. Apparently, David Taylor found the medallion among several human ribs—a fact that appears to have troubled the boy.

"He grew increasingly nervous as the weeks passed," Lorraine told me. "He had always been a very good student, but suddenly he was having trouble concentrating on his homework. I know he was having nightmares, and he seemed to be obsessed with thoughts of Indians. It really bothered him that he'd dug up a grave."

Lorraine also had nightmares. In one, she and her son were standing in water up to their necks. The boy held the gold medallion in his hand. Then he dropped it. She begged him not to go after it, but he laughed and disappeared beneath the water's surface.

Three days after she experienced this dream, David Taylor hanged himself from a tree.

It's a tragic story that gets worse. While still out of her mind with grief, Lorraine was approached by a local amateur treasure hunter who told her that if she would be willing to participate in a séance at his house, it might be possible for her to communicate with her dead son. She agreed to attend.

At the séance, Lorraine, the treasure hunter, and several other participants sat looking at a candle as David "spoke" from the grave through a series of small raps on the table. The boy was asked whether his mother should give the medallion to the treasure hunter. Two raps—yes. Lorraine did as she was told.

But life did not go smoothly for the treasure hunter once he took possession of the ancient artifact. When the news got around about how he'd hoodwinked Lorraine, the community was so outraged that he decided to move away. Later, he would sell the medallion, saying, "I'm glad to get rid of the damn thing."

The man who bought it lives within a few hundred yards of the area where the medallion was found, and he had his share of problems with the Calusa medallion, too.

"A friend and I bought it just to get it away from the guy who cheated David's mother," he once explained. "We gave it to a third friend, with the stipulation that it be placed in a museum with David's name on it. But our friend was worried that publicly displaying it would only promote more looting. Eventually, we began to bicker. One friend purchased the other friend's share. We bickered some more. It came so close to ruining our friendship that we began to joke about it. The Curse of the Medallion, we called it."

The owner once told a reporter, "I'm not superstitious. But I've given the thing away three times, and each time it's ended up back in my hands. My Indian friends—who are superstitious—say that's because the medallion is meant to remain here. They say it should be reburied."

The owner did rebury it—until he ultimately donated it to the Florida Museum of Natural History.

I know because the owner was me.

"Discussing a find as rare as David Taylor's is a double-edged sword," Marquardt said. "When we publicize information about archaeological artifacts, we risk more damage to the mounds. On the other hand, the more people we educate about how much can be learned from the sites, the better chance we have that people will want to protect them."

We were now twenty-five miles from Fort Myers, roaming around the bayside village of Pineland on Pine Island, which is connected by a drawbridge to the mainland. The mounds around Pineland are among the Florida Museum of Natural History's most important and ambitious projects and may offer the last best hope for understanding the Calusa.

In 1895, the Pineland sites were first described by Smithsonian ethnologist Frank Hamilton Cushing: "The foundations, graded ways, and canals here were greater . . . than any I had yet seen. The central courts were enormous."

The ruins have remained relatively unscathed since Cushing's time, but as looters have become more and more brazen in recent years, Marquardt fears that the sites are increasingly vulnerable.

"A few years ago," he said, "three men were arrested for using a bulldozer—a bulldozer!—on one of the remote islands. They were using it to dig up the mounds. They completely destroyed one of the area's most important sites. And you know why? They said they were looking for 'José Gaspar's treasure.' It would be laughable if it wasn't so tragic."

Laughable because José Gaspar was invented out of whole cloth in 1919 by a railroad company flack who needed a way to romanticize the mosquito-infested area in order to promote both tourism and land sales along what he called "the pirate coast."

That the west coast of Florida was far off the route of Spanish gold shipments (and thus had no pirates) did not deter later Gaspar "historians," whose cheap fabrications are still on sale in Florida bookstores. Many of the booklets contain "authentic" pirate maps where X marks the spot—and the spot is always an Indian mound.

The fiction of Gaspar and his "captive women" has been so widely accepted that Tampa has an annual José Gaspar Festival.

"The treasure is mythical," Marquardt said, "but the hope is persistent. The story's always the same. The treasure's buried next to a gumbo limbo tree on one of the mounds. Every year, new people hear those stories, and they think, 'Hey, I'm going to get my buddies and do some digging.'"

Other relic hounds have struck out in the hope of unearthing more medallions like the one David Taylor found.

"I think the whole story of the medallion is tragic," Marquardt said as we stood on a bluff at the Pineland site, looking out across a vast courtyard toward another shell pyramid. "It's tragic what happened to the boy, and it's tragic that artifact hunters have been trying to duplicate his find."

Marquardt pointed to an old crater in the shellwork—not even Pineland had been spared. "If there's a curse," he said, "you're looking at it."

The Big Queasy

———••——

RECENTLY I WAS FORCED TO NOTIFY the Human Movement and Balance Unit of the United Kingdom's Medical Research Council that I would not be delivering my much-anticipated paper at its International Workshop on Motion Sickness in Portugal.

True, the paper I had hoped to present was anticipated mostly by me. But still I feel like I've failed the scientific community—not to mention those wretched souls who, out of personal weakness and lack of grit, foul this republic's waterways and airsickness bags in a selfish attempt to leverage sympathy.

As I explained to Dr. Angus H. Rupert of the Naval Aerospace Medical Research Laboratory in Pensacola, Florida, "Commander, I once believed that compassion plus certain homeopathic prophylaxes were the only keys to dealing with people who are prone to motion sickness. I was wrong. These people are hopeless. They deserve whatever the hell happens to them."

Dr. Rupert—who, surprisingly, had never heard of me or my work—replied, "I take it that your experiment failed."

Did it ever. In the space of a single boat trip, all my carefully constructed theories about motion sickness crumbled. "You and the other American researchers will have to go to Portugal without me," I told Dr. Rupert. "Please pass along my apologies—I've let you all down."

By taking the high road and accepting the blame, I was fulfilling my professional obligation to protect the anonymity of the real culprit, a certain man named James W. Hall. A tenured professor of creative writing and literature at Florida International University in Miami, Hall is a highly regarded poet and author of such best-selling eco-thrillers as *Gone Wild, Bones of Coral, Under Cover of Daylight, Buzz Cut,* and *Blackwater Sound.* About his work, the *New York Times Book Review* once stated, "James W. Hall's writing runs as clean and fast as the Gulf Stream waters." Obviously, the reviewer had never been in the Gulf Stream in a boat that was down-current from Jim Hall.

Months ago, when I was interviewing candidates for my seasickness experiment, Hall told me, "I think my mother seeded the idea of motion sickness in me when I was a child. On the first long car trip our family ever took, she said, 'I don't want you getting carsick!' It had never occurred to me to get carsick. I didn't even know what carsickness was. Then my mother said, 'Whatever you do, don't watch those telephone lines.' What would any child do? I lay down in the backseat and watched the phone lines go up and down, up and down, up . . . and . . . down." Hall suddenly stopped talking and took several deep gulps of air. "Can we change the subject?" he asked. "I'd really like to change the subject."

I found it interesting to see how Hall abjured all personal responsibility for his weakness by fronting the despicable fiction that it was his mother's fault—transference, those of us in the profession call it. "That's one of the most pathetic stories I've ever heard," I said to him. "Please tell me more."

He did, and it got better. "The first time I became seasick," he said, "was in a friend's boat off Key Largo. It got a little choppy and my friend said, 'Hope you don't get seasick.' That's all it took. I spent the next hour being unwell."

"Unwell" is a favorite euphemism of the many literary types who suffer *mal de mer*; they use it in an attempt to distance themselves from blue-collar terms such as "commode vespers" and "stomach flute serenade." The preferred scientific term, "bilging ship," is almost never used.

"The next time I got sick was off Key West," Hall told me. "I'd been assigned by a magazine to cover a marlin fishing tournament. It was twelve hours of absolute hell. My knees were bloody by the time we docked. No fish were caught, so I wrote about the existential quandary of being unwell while everyone else on the boat is eating chicken."

The man's litany of humiliations was impressive indeed, but what made him an ideal research subject was this curious fact: Benny W. Hall owns a boat.

Would a claustrophobe purchase a cave? Would an acrophobe spend weekends dangling from a bungee-jumping tower? It told me that Hall had spunk. His explanation confirmed it. "I hate being sick, but I like to fish. I love to be on the water. I've tried Dramamine, but it just knocks me out. And then I get sick anyway. The ear patch, the acupressure wristband—nothing works. But I refuse to be bullied. I take the boat out every chance I get."

Hall was perfect: a poet who approached his affliction with the sensibilities of a foundry town linebacker. Still, it wasn't easy to convince him that I held the key to his recovery. "What makes you think you understand seasickness?" he asked. "You've never been seasick in your life."

He was right on that score. But I had been a fishing guide for many years, and I'd seen hundreds of Hall's desperate kindred abandoning all pretense of human dignity before heaven and anyone dumb enough to watch. No one could doubt that I wasn't sympathetic.

"I'm a licensed captain," I replied. "A professional, for God's sake. I've watched mature adults perform like Veg-O-Matics, then crawl off my skiff without tipping. I once returned from Mariel Harbor, Cuba, with a boat full of 147 puking refugees. I don't understand seasickness? What I understand is that you people make the mess but never stick around to help clean up. Which is why I've dedicated so much time to devising a cure."

"And you've found one?" Hall asked.

I answered, "Why don't we take your boat out into the Gulf Stream and see for ourselves? What do you have to lose that you wouldn't lose anyway?"

THE EVENING BEFORE OUR TRIP, I planned to have Hall follow a carefully devised routine that included eating all the spaghetti he wanted. The next morning, before heading out, he would consume a breakfast of chocolate-chip cookies. Then, as a counterbalance, he would take some ginger capsules, which are thought by some to be a seasickness preventive. "I'm not sure I can do this," he said when I outlined the regimen. "God, how I hate the sound of my own retching!"

"I didn't mention the cotton?" I said. "You're not going to hear anything, because you'll have cotton in your ears."

Admittedly, my approach to curing motion sickness flew in the face of the scientific community. I knew this to be true, because I had read the research and interviewed several of this country's leading authorities.

It's generally accepted that the symptoms of motion sickness begin when the brain receives confusing messages from the inner ear. Responsible for the body's balance mechanism, the inner ear contains certain calcium crystals, known as otoliths, that are designed to tell the brain whether or not the head is level. But otoliths can be un-trustworthy when one's environment goes topsy-turvy. The inner ear also has tubes, called semicircular canals, filled with a fluid that sloshes back and forth with every rise and fall of a boat, plane, or car. Frustrated by all this chaotic data, the brain may choose to seek revenge (no one can explain why) by punishing the spirit. First, body temperature drops and the skin pales. Then the level of vasopressin, a hormone, rises in the bloodstream as the sufferer experiences cold sweats and uncontrollable salivation.

The final stage is nausea and a God-honest yearning to return to the womb, which is why so many motion sickness victims pray for death from a fetal position. Oddly, there are people who are fine during the course of a trip, only to suffer all the symptoms once on solid ground. *Mal d'embarquement,* the malady is called.

"SOME PEOPLE GET SICK VERY EASILY," Dr. Deborah Harm, a senior neuroscientist at the Johnson Space Center in Houston, told me. "With others, it takes a strenuous laboratory procedure to create symptoms. The only people who are immune are those with a nonfunctional vestibular system, which means inner-ear damage due to disease."

Disease? Slightly irritated, I pointed out to Dr. Harm that my vestibular system was full of life and as functional as anyone's. "Well," she said (cryptically, I felt), "it's also true that psychological components can play a part."

Dr. Rupert told me that certain types of people were more prone to the malady. "The very young and the very old seem to be more susceptible," he said. "Research also suggests that women are more susceptible than men. And there is a correlation between people who are aerobically fit and motion sickness. That is, if you're in very good shape, you have a slightly better chance of getting sick than if you're some couch potato."

THIS WAS VERY GOOD NEWS for couch fixture Jim Hall—and I told him so on a Saturday morning at the Black Point Marina on Biscayne Bay, just south of Miami. We had Hall's twenty-foot Mako in the water. The cooler was packed with ice, sandwiches, and beverages. The bait locker was loaded with fresh-dead ballyhoo, a small, needle-nosed fish, for trolling. "I want this experiment to be as true to life as possible," I told Hall and his friend, Joe Wisdom, as we idled through the canal toward the Atlantic. "Forget that I'm making extensive notes on your every move. Just do what you normally do on a typical fishing trip."

"Normally," Wisdom said, checking his watch, "I have a beer about now."

Gad! It wasn't quite 9 A.M. Wisdom, though a respected dean at Florida International, had the look of a mean and unpredictable drunk. But because he is an expert fisherman, I had invited him along to run the boat and also to serve as a control subject. Not prone to motion sickness, Wisdom had been fed spaghetti the night before but had not been given ginger capsules.

I sat at the stern of the Mako, cutting the lard-soft ballyhoo into chunks as Wisdom powered the boat onto plane and steered us across the bay. Then it was out through the cut at Boca Chita and into the Gulf Stream, where more expensive Miami lunches have been lost than to any combination of spring-break toga parties and swine flu. Up to my elbows in gore, I waved Hall toward me. "Been eating lots of cookies? You take your ginger capsules?"

Hall responded, "Huh?"

I reached up, yanked the cotton out of his ears, and repeated the questions.

He nodded: Yes, he'd done both.

"I hate to break it to you, but those ginger pills are useless. Studies have shown that they're absolute quackery. I'm telling you this now because the only way you can spare yourself is to immedi-ately change your attitude about seasickness."

I thought Hall was going to punch me. "You set me up, you spawn! I suppose the cotton balls are a lie, too!"

Before I could answer, he'd thrown them overboard. As I watched them sink, I said, "No-o-o-o, the cotton balls could have saved you. Very soothing to the inner ear. Your only hope now is to follow my directions to the letter. Remember: You have a bellyful of Italian food."

Hall wisely decided to listen.

"After years of careful observation," I said, "I've come to the conclusion that you people make yourselves sick with your constant fretting. Tell the truth: Haven't you spent the whole morning wor-rying about getting sick?"

"My wife did say I looked a little pale when I left the house," Hall admitted.

"That's why you have to change your mental approach from de-fense to offense. Go on the attack! You have to try to get sick. Re-verse your cerebral polarity and you'll never have another unwell day in your life."

"Try to get sick?" Hall considered it for a moment. "That's plain stupid. Besides, it's too nice a day to get sick. I think I'm going to be just fine today."

It was a nice day. Dead calm. To the northwest was the stalag-mite clutter of Miami's skyscrapers. Behind us were the shoals of Biscayne Bay. Ahead was the violet demarcation of the Gulf Stream. It, too, was dead calm.

With Hall refusing to cooperate, I was forced to take more ex-treme measures to keep the experiment on track. I wiped my hands on my shirt and pulled out a box of Nicaraguan cigars from the bag at my feet. "I really didn't want to have to use these," I said.

I've never been a smoker, nor will I ever be. Perhaps that is why the hour that followed is a little blurry. Joe Wisdom, serving as our guide, located a school of dolphin fish. We caught a couple while trolling and then cut the engine to sight-cast. Every few minutes I'd toss out a glob of chum to keep the school close. We drifted along, rolling and rocking on a weak sea, catching one fish after another. Soon the deck was a mess of blood and flopping dolphins.

I was so busy fishing and chumming and smoking that I'd almost forgotten about Hall when I heard a shaky, childlike voice moan, "Oh my . . . oh my . . . " Hall was collapsed on the console seat, his head in his hands. He looked up at me for a brief moment. His face was the color of rancid tallow. "Isn't it hot out here? I feel really hot."

I removed my cigar. "You're not hot, you milksop. You're seasick—this close to bilging ship. And all because you didn't take my advice. Now I'm going to have to start from square one." I puffed on the cigar, which by now was saturated with ballyhoo juice. For the first time, I noticed that the thing had a very odd odor, not unlike a can of bad tuna that has been stored in a cedar chest. I sniffed at the cigar, then tossed it into the garbage bucket.

I noticed, also, that I had broken out in a cold sweat. Meanwhile, my eyes had found an unexpected focus: all that fish offal coating the boat. When I tried to divert my attention, my eyes swung inexorably back to the deck. To Wisdom, I said, "Is the wind picking up? It feels to me like the wind's starting to pick up."

Wisdom, who was finishing his umpteenth beer, replied, "There's no wind. A little groundswell, that's all."

Groundswell, no doubt. Long, rolling waves that lifted the boat, then dropped it. One after another—bow up, stern down, stern up, bow down. "Know something?" I said to Hall. "It *is* hot out here."

Hall was hunched over, holding his stomach, muttering something about Italian food. I wiped my face on my hands. The smell of that cigar was everywhere. "Whew!" I said. "Scoot over. All that chumming has made my legs tired."

Hall looked up long enough to say, "You know, you don't look so good."

"Shut up and mind your own affairs," I snapped. "All your whining is making me queasy." Then, to Wisdom, I called, "Can't you make this boat stop rocking?"

Wisdom, oblivious to it all, was hunched over the cooler. "Hey," he said, "who drank all the beer? If we're out of beer, then I think we should head in."

I was sweating, and feeling what I now prefer to call unwell. "Of course we should head in!" I shouted. "Hall refuses to play along with the experiment. And besides, I think I may be getting a touch of the flu."

Which is precisely why I won't be presenting my paper to the International Workshop on Motion Sickness in Portugal.

THE BACK OF BEYOND

As I WRITE THIS I AM SEVERAL BEERS into a nine-hour layover at Los Angeles International Airport, which is where the travel agent who booked this goat-fest should be clove hitched shoeless among the stampeding new arrivals from Phnom Penh, New Delhi, and other cauldrons of Asia.

Have I mentioned that I am just a tad grumpy? Yes, indeed— grumpy and severely jet-lagged after another whirlwind visit to the far side of the earth. In the last many years, how many times have I crossed the Pacific? Lots. But of all those flights, this trip has been the dead-rump hell tour from Planet Dumbo, put together by a travel agency in Missouri that appears to have less foresight than roadkill in Amish country. On every leg of every flight, I was booked into a center seat. Not an aisle or bulkhead seat on the whole rotten journey, and that includes both fourteen-hour legs between LAX and Sydney. Spend three full working days sandwiched between fat men who stink of curry and fat women who smell of their curry-bloated men and it's the rare mood ring that won't turn black.

There's another reason I might be a tad grumpy. Over the hundred months that I've written this column outside, I've undoubtedly had the best gig in the business. I've traveled several hundred thousand miles to dozens of countries on assignments that just about any writer would have died for—but that were assigned to me instead. And now, as I write what will be my very last "Out There" column, I find it especially irksome to have to do so against the backdrop of this sad place.

So, no, I'm not in the best of humors. But these four beers have helped. Really cold beer, too, served up by my new buddy Mark, the bartender. As this wise little man has already pointed out, I'm on an expense account, so why not have a little fun.

"Another?" he asks.

"I'll sail again," I tell him with a nod, and then return my attention to the blue-gray illumination of my PowerBook.

I like that line: "I'll sail again." In *The Sands of Iwo Jima,* John Wayne's corporal, Forrest Tucker, always uses it to order another round. The phrase has a certain 1940s last-flight-out charm that's happily at odds with the sterile nineties decor of the place where I now sit.

Where I now sit is the plush, members-only Admirals Club of American Airlines. Since I'm not a member, the less said about how I gained entrance, the better. Mark doesn't know, nor do the two women guarding the front desk. It shouldn't have been so easy to finesse, especially considering that I'm dressed in my standard travel kit: khaki fishing shorts, T-shirt, and ball cap. But here I am, with the run of the place.

The LAX Admirals Club isn't nearly as nice as the Qantas Upper Deck lounges I've crashed over the years, but it's OK, functionally impressive with its burgundy faux-leather seats and carpeted enclaves equipped with computers and fax machines. Spending nine hours here is much better than sitting downstairs in Concourse Two. Even so, I can't stand the boredom and the waste of time. Hanging around in airports is the thing I hate most about travel.

Wait a minute . . . Is that true? Let me think about this a little more. It's an interesting question, an aspect of my work I've never before tried to pin to the floor. What do I dislike *most* about travel? In my present mood, the notion of zeroing in on this matter appeals to a certain perversity of spirit, one that has been exacerbated by all this delicious beer. Let me inspect the larger canvas. Let me review all the years, all the trips, all the disturbing, vexing encounters, and make some quick, cryptic notes. Those Peruvian goons who stabbed me . . . Lost and near tears on Old Baldy . . . A spider, a broom, and that bastard honey bucket . . . The oldest orangutan trick in the book . . . Rats and mefloquine demons in Hanoi . . . The garbage children of Guatemala . . . Dope smuggling tarpon fiends in Singapore . . . You're not drunk, you're in Borneo . . . The crappiest airplane terminal in the world . . .

Hmmm. It's a list that could go on and on, but here is what I've just noticed: Instead of filling me with angst, or dread, or revulsion, a quick review of even my worst trips brings a little smile to my face. It's the kind of smile that indicates a slight thoracic pressure, as if one's heart is being squeezed, but it's a smile all the same. There's a reason: I can't dredge up an unhappy event without remembering the country in which it took place and more important, the people who, without fail, befriended me.

"You just think about something funny?" Mark the bartender pauses to inquire. I don't answer.

Mark clears his throat nervously. Rote ceremony is the scaffolding upon which all uneasy alliances rely. "More pretzels, sir?" he asks, already moving away.

Nope. No more of those pretzels, and no more of those shiny pea-looking whatchamacallits, either. No thanks. But I will have another beer.

When most people look at a map, they see geography. When I look at a map, I see people. Australia? I see Neville Walker and his sons. Or Bryan Price, who's keeping baseball healthy in the land Down Under. I see the shape of Cuba, and I think of Blas Mesa, or an amazing pitcher, The Man With a Hundred Moves. Costa Rica—it's my brilliant friend Bayardo Orochena. Little Cayman Island: Sam McCoy and his wife, Mary. Panama? Don't get me started on Panama.

The point is, in every country I've visited, whether it's Mexico, Peru, Colombia, Ireland, the Philippines, Sumatra, Nicaragua, or wherever, there were good men and women who recognized me for the absentminded goof I am and who gladly took me under their wings. And so, ironically enough, here's my answer: The thing I dislike most about travel is meeting people. You heard me right. It's interacting with other fine souls in far-off, isolated places, usually under intimate and intense circumstances, and then having to say good-bye.

Le Hui Vu comes immediately to mind. Vu was my guide when I visited Vietnam in January of 1992. Because this was before the U.S. embargo had been lifted, I had to enter the country illegally, but Vu didn't much care. In terms of life experiences, dealing with minor illegalities was small potatoes to Vu. He'd spent fifteen years in the jungle fighting with the Communist Vietcong San, 320 Division, Seventh Frontier Guerrillas.

"Ve-ly famous to Americans!" he told me. "And ve-ly dangerous."

Vu had tiny brown pit-bull eyes but the demeanor of a boy who'd aged into adulthood without being ingested by it. He was small and round and genial, but possessed a depth of character and experience not implied by his appearance.

For instance, Vu had been with the main contingent of Vietcong

that, on the eve of the 1968 Tet Offensive, captured the Citadel at
Hue and held off the U.S. Marines for nearly a month before
retreating under darkness—and after executing more than three
thousand civilians, whose bodies they left behind in shallow graves.

That was something else he told me, but only after we had pro-
gressed from acquaintances to close friends. And Vu and I became
close friends very, very quickly. Aside from the fact that we were
both dedicated fathers, our only link was generational, but it's my
experience that friendship has more to do with alchemy than anything else, so there's no explaining it. I liked and trusted Vu; he liked
and trusted me. When we were off by ourselves, we'd joke around
and giggle like kids. I called him Mr. Vu. He called me Mr. Wandy.

In Hue, he escorted me around the sacred temple where he and
the other Vietcong had fought, showed me old bullet scars, and explained various fields of fire. He also showed me how they escaped
under cover of darkness and where they had buried the civilians they
had killed. It was an eerie, odd experience, part expository, part con-
fession. A profound sadness washed over his face. More than once
we got teary-eyed together.

But Vu's favorite pastime was getting me lost in the rain forest,
sneaking around close behind, and surprising me by whispering,
"Bang, bang, you dead."

To which I would promptly reply, "Fuck you, Vu."

A response that made him giggle some more. "No thank you,"
he'd answer. "Ve-ly kind, but not intah-lested."

When I left Vietnam, I thought that was the end of my relationship with Vu, but it wasn't. He wrote and sent pictures. I wrote
back. In the earliest hours of the morning, I've been awakened
more than once to hear the faint echo of his voice: "Hello, Mr.
Wandy! Hello!"

Stranger still is the number of people, American and Vietnamese, whom through one extraordinary coincidence or another I have met because we are all friends of Vu. This is another oddity I've noticed about certain rare friendships that evolve on the road: They happen so quickly and are so intense that they seem to generate an energy of their own, one so potent that time and distance are inconsequential.

My friend Dean Fallsdown is a good example. I met Dean at a diner while writing about the crystal-huggers of Sedona, Arizona. "How do you deal with all these New Agers?" I asked this decidedly ungroovy American Indian man.

"I tell them I'm Jewish," he replied.

We became friends immediately, and I soon learned that he was a medicine man at the nearby Yavapai Apache reservation. Dean invited me to a tribal sweat ceremony—a very sociable, nonmystical experience in which I thought I would faint, but didn't. Thereafter Dean would call me every few months to talk. In one conversation, he told me that the members of his tribe believed that a sacred artifact, stolen back in the 1950s, was somewhere in my home state of Florida. "We'd like you to find it," he said.

I explained to Dean that Florida is a big place and that forty years is a long time, but that I'd try to make a few calls to artifact collectors. And I did place some calls, though I turned up nothing.

Not long after that, Dean called me again. "Hey," he said. "Randy, we want to thank you. We got the artifact back."

It turned out that an Orlando collector I'd called—a man who claimed to have no knowledge of the artifact—had suddenly suffered a bout of conscience and returned the artifact to Dean's tribe.

"Amazing," I said.

Dean didn't think so. He was underwhelmed, in fact, by the several coincidences and freak encounters that we experienced during our friendship. I found such coincidences both heartening and a little troubling, perhaps because I'm a linear person, a man who's not even tempted to read his own horoscope in the paper. Yet last year, when I was going through some interesting romantic problems, it was Dean I called on for advice.

"We'll get together in December," he said. "That's when I'll be able to help you." December? I had no plans to be in Arizona in December. Was Dean coming to Florida? "You'll see," he said. "There's going to be a ceremony. After December, you'll be OK."

All of which turned out to be pretty much the truth. Later that winter, when I called to tell him about my strong recovery, Dean wasn't around. He'd died, of natural causes. In December.

And that is the very worst thing about travel. You befriend people on far-off continents and maybe even fall in love with the idea of staying there and living the disconnected life. It's not because you're unhappy with your old life back home. No, that has nothing to do with it. You project yourself onto this new place, fantasize about an existence there, mostly because the people you've met are so dear that you don't want to leave. But you always do leave. Which is why it squeezes the heart to see a map or spin a globe. Because the more places you go, the more people you end up missing.

It's the same with writing this column. The energy that drives the weird beast, Out There, is really generated by you, its readers. You don't know it. Hell, you probably wouldn't admit it if you did, and I don't blame you. But it's true, and I want to thank you for helping me validate a stray-dog approach to travel that seems to infuriate more orderly, tight-sphinctered types. It's been the best gig in the business, and I'm going to miss it.

What I won't miss is hellishly long layovers like this nine-hour marathon in LAX. But sometimes you've got to suck it up and make the best of things. It's like I just told Mark: I'll sail again.

THE LIGHTNING STALKER
STRIKES AGAIN

————•·•————

BECAUSE WE'RE STANDING in an open field near Orlando, Florida, because thunderheads are boiling toward us, because the first cold breath of the storm has alerted my bushman's survival instincts, I feel it's important to review for the Lightning Stalker certain incidents that illustrate the long-standing animus between me, my family, and demon electricity.

"Remember the story I told you?" I yell over the howling wind. "The story about what happened when I lived on the farm?"

Preoccupied, the Lightning Stalker says, "Huh? What?" He has positioned himself in the middle of the field. He has his old Minolta camera mounted on a Bogen tripod, lens focused on the towering clouds. The shutter cord is in his hand, ready to fire, and he peers up at the sky through thick eyeglasses. With his beard and hippie-length hair blowing wild in the wind, the Lightning Stalker appears crazed with delight. In the strobing dusk, he looks a little too much like Moses for comfort.

He turns briefly to speak. "You mean when you peed on that electric fence? That's wild stuff, man! But, hey, I'm sorta busy right now."

I'd been far more delicate in explaining the unfortunate occurrence: A sensitive, inexperienced boy. A bull paddock enclosed by wire through which flowed some very serious voltage. An impromptu beverage-chugging contest. The pause to void, the playful sweep of hips.

"It really hurt," I tell him.

"I bet it did, man!"

"Psychologically, I mean."

"Sure, runs right up the spine to the brain. We're electric creatures!"

Exactly right—the low-amperage variety. Which is why all my instincts tell me that I should now be huddled in the Lightning Stalker's Jeep Wagoneer, parked a hundred yards away from here, rather than standing out in a field with this madman while doom descends.

"Now she's really starting to cook!" he says. Two big storm cells, iridescent against the setting sun, are blowing toward us, feeding on the flatland heat of central Florida. We can feel the artillery rumble of thunder through a conduit of cooling air and earth, can hear the thunder's pitch gradually ascending as the storms grow nearer. There is a vein of light, and my companion begins to count aloud. Twenty seconds later, we hear the thunder. "Five seconds to a mile!" he yells. "She's closing. I've got to get to work."

For the last twenty years, the Lightning Stalker has stood out in storms like this one, risking life and limb to photograph electricity. He's an artist, and like most artists, he can think only of his own selfish wants. Never mind the point that I'm trying to make.

"You know, that story about my great-grandfather . . . "

"Yeah, you told me that one. The preacher, right?"

Yes, a North Carolina circuit preacher. A respected citizen of the state and the father of eight children, this holy man fell victim to desires of the flesh. One night he packed his organ-player mistress into a wagon, and the two of them galloped toward the godless north. Upon crossing the Virginia border, my great-grandfather was struck and killed by lightning.

"It's absolutely true," I shout. "I've got a copy of the death certificate to prove it!" Inching toward the Wagoneer, I add, "That's why I should go back and sit in the car. Electricity hates us. The entire family's cursed."

The Lightning Stalker is focused on the storm, working the camera's shutter, counting: "Thousand-one, thousand-two, thousand-three . . . "

I'm now speaking over my shoulder, in slow retreat. "It's one of those generational deals. Apparently God's still miffed about the whole business. If He decides to take another potshot at me, you could get nailed by the shrapnel."

I hear the Lightning Stalker yell, "WOW!" in response to a burst of celestial light, a deafening blast of thunder. Instantly I'm sprinting toward the car, running a serpentine pattern, yelling words the Lightning Stalker may or may not hear: "I'm only doing this for you!"

"Confront your fears—just don't be stupid about it," the Lightning Stalker told me when I telephoned to ask if I could tag along on a trip. "You're afraid of lightning? Good. I'll trust you to carry my gear."

The Lightning Stalker is named David O. Stillings, and he's from Winter Springs, which is just north of Orlando and the Magic Kingdom. He describes his part of Florida as "the lightning capital of North America," in a tone that communicates a mixture of pride and private reality: He lives in the belly of his own chosen beast.

"Lightning is the last dinosaur, man!" he says. "It's got a mind. It's alive!"

If lightning isn't alive, it's certainly lively. Some interesting facts:

At any given time about two thousand thunderstorms may exist worldwide, producing lightning flashes at a total rate of one hundred per second. The peak temperature of a lightning bolt—in excess of 50,000 degrees—is four times hotter than the surface of the sun. Lighting does strike twice in the same place—more than twice, sometimes—and it does indeed have its favorite targets. My great-grandfather was one. The Empire State Building is another; it's been hit as many as forty-eight times in a single year.

Stillings has never been directly hit by lightning, but he says he's been blasted off the ground more than once. "It's a lot better than the life I was living," he reasons. "That should tell you something."

It does. In 1976, Stillings was broke, dispirited, and going nowhere fast. He'd washed out of the navy. A prolific poet, he'd failed to find a publisher for even one of his poems. Then one afternoon a fore-token of his life's work appeared in the rearview mirror of his '64 Olds convertible.

"I was driving around with the top down," he says. "I had a camera, because I wanted to take a picture of the sunset. And there it was—boom—a bolt of lightning in the mirror. I believe in stuff like that. We all get signs that can take us down really neat paths. I did a U-turn, and this storm was beautiful. I started taking pictures. I'm telling you, it was an adrenaline rush. It was me."

That was more than 150,000 miles and 80,000 photographs ago. Since that day, Stillings, who is now forty-eight years old, has dedicated his life to his craft. "If I was rich, people would call me eccentric. As it is, people just say I'm obsessed."

He scoffs at certain western states—Arizona, for example—that also claim to be the lightning capital. "Oh sure, it's easier to photograph lightning out west," he says. "Just drive up any mountain and shoot across a valley—everything's safe and dry. But central Florida is dead-center in the flight path of all the storms that come in from the Gulf and the Atlantic. Monster storms, man."

Stillings says he shoots lightning in the purest, most honest way he can. That means going into the teeth of a developing storm cell, waiting it out, shooting it raw. It also means no camera tricks, no filters, and no lengthy time exposures. "If I leave the shutter open for more than three seconds, I start feeling guilty about it. Sure, it'd guarantee I'd get lightning, but I'd also lose color and cloud detail. All that ambient light just eats up the negative." In a year, Stillings will shoot 4,000 photographs. Out of that, he might get twelve images that he can use but maybe only one or two that he's really proud of.

"I'm telling you," he says, "it's a full-time job."

Which is why Stillings, broke when he started, is still broke. His wife, Judy, a hearing-aid specialist, provides income for the cause. He sells his photographs through Black Oak Art Studio in nearby Casselberry, and he might make $3,000 in a good year. "Money for film and gas," he says. "That's all I need."

His work has been featured in a number of galleries around the state. Epcot Center even invited him to do a show. Stillings has also traded his photographs for a few niceties. "I once traded lightning for a used clothes washer and dryer. I traded lightning for a television. I traded lightning for my Wagoneer." He also traded lightning for a used transmission to get the Wagoneer running.

Over the years, Stillings has become a well-known fixture in his region: a lone man with camera, confronting storms in open fields, from rooftops, from any place where the angle is good and thunder is popping. Locals dubbed him the Lightning Stalker. His friends even had a rain slicker made with the moniker in big white letters stretching across the back. "That's so I wouldn't get hassled by the cops so much," he explains. "If it's a dark night out and you're roaming around private property in a big rainstorm, the police will tend to draw their weapons before asking questions. And who can blame them?"

Stillings, in short, is a member of a small, twisted American fraternity of heavy-weather chasers, one of those rare people who are driven to seek clarity in the midst of chaos. Some of them pursue tornadoes. Some of them park themselves in the path of hurricanes. A few of the crazier ones chase lightning.

"Yeah, I'm crazy," he told me on the phone. "But I'm positive crazy, not negative crazy. I don't have a death wish. I like to go around to schools and show my slides, rap with the kids. I try to educate them about what lightning is, tell them how to avoid it. To me, that's being positive crazy. I don't drink, I don't smoke, and I don't use drugs. Lightning's my whole life. If you really want to get to know the beast, man, you're more than welcome to ride with me."

That's how I came to be standing in an open field with the Lightning Stalker, watching doom descend, struggling to confront my fears.

Between a hundred and two hundred people are killed by lightning every year in the United States. Lightning is the direct cause of more deaths than snowstorms, tornadoes, hurricanes, floods, and deranged postal employees. It's personal. It's the Creator's version of an early-admissions system: zap, and you move on to the next level.

I remind myself of that as I sit in the Wagoneer, watching Stillings do his work. No fool, he's hunkered down low. He has a bottle of Mountain Dew in one hand, the shutter cable in the other. It's dark enough now so that I can see him clearly only when there's a blast of lightning. Same with the clouds: They have formed a mountainous amphitheater around us and the banks of Lake Apopka, near which we are located.

On the drive from his home, Stillings said, "Storms feed on warmth, like an alien ship gobbling up energy."

Yeah, the guy's a *Star Trek* fan, but in this case he's right. The storm has vacuumed away all the heat and wind, leaving the night air cool. In the void, the stillness is tinged with eerie light, bile-green and chrome. I open the door and step out experimentally to test one of the Lightning Stalker's claims: "Just before a big storm hits, have you ever noticed there are no mosquitoes? They just disappear. It's true. Animals can sense when the lid's about to blow off."

I stand there anticipating the insect whine. A still night in Florida without mosquitoes is oxymoronic, but the guy's right again. No mosquitoes. A little later, I feel the stirring breeze and the first fat drops of rain. Stillings is running toward me, carrying his gear.

"Time to move!" he yells. "Water and my lenses don't mix!"

I ask, "We're done for the night?"

"No way. Just getting started. I know where this storm is headed. What we do now is drive southeast, set up, and wait on it again. Did you notice the edges of those clouds? When the tops of clouds have real sharp edges, the storm's still building. Fuzzy edges mean the storm's dying. This thing's getting stronger." He throws his fists above his head. "I mean, WOW!"

Like an alien ship himself, the Lightning Stalker seems to be gobbling energy from the storm. As we drive Highway 441 through tiny Plymouth toward the city of Apopka, he performs a nonstop monologue, his thought process leaping from branch to progressively smaller branch.

"You know why I keep my hair so long? 'Cause when it comes to lightning, hair's an early warning system. People think rubber tires will insulate a car from the ground. No way. Yeah, a car's pretty safe, because lightning will follow the metal body to ground, but the tires have nothing to do with it. Same with wearing rubber shoes— no help at all. After traveling 30,000 feet through insulating air, the beast will not be halted by half an inch of rubber. And trees? Can you believe people still run to trees for cover? Fifteen percent of the people killed by lightning are standing under trees."

As we bounce into another field to watch the advancing storm all over again, I tell the Lightning Stalker that this time I'm not getting out.

"No sense both of us being struck dead," I explain. "One of us should be in the Jeep, ready to go for help at a moment's notice."

The Lightning Stalker is collecting his gear, his face turned skyward so that the distant light show flickers in his glasses. "The Wagoneer?" he asks, smiling. "Sounds just like your great-granddad. Yeah, man—stay in the wagon."

No More Curse of
the Sheepherders

---

*In memory of Sir Peter Blake, a great traveler, a brilliant
Kiwi sailor, and a good and decent man.*

ALL THINGS CONSIDERED, the best place for a journalist to watch
the finals of America's Cup XXIX was Auckland, New Zealand, not
San Diego, particularly if the journalist was an American who, in
eight years of applying loose cover to the event, had yet to decipher
why any child of his republic should give a hoot in hell about a
144-year-old yacht race that is won or lost in a laboratory test tank,
then played out as maritime theater by people who, historically,
have been fops, snobs, and litigious eels.

Yes, Auckland was the place. Maybe stroll among Waitemata
Harbor's umpteen thousand sailboats, then order eggs with snarlers
at the Loaded Hog Pub and watch the races on the big screen above
the bar. Kick back with the locals and pound down beverages, even
though New Zealand's television coverage would begin at 9 A.M.,

37

the breakfast hour for outsiders but the first cool vent of the Stein-lager window for a hard-core Kiwi.

On off days, drive up to Lake Taupo and do some brown-trout fishing; eat Vegemite and biscuits in the shade, looking out across a landscape that has been manicured as neatly as the twelfth green of Augusta by clouds of grazing sheep. This was incentive enough, but being 6,000 miles from San Diego's Point Loma also meant there was absolutely no chance I would find myself ducking upchuck on the Official Press Boat—or at the Media Center, for that matter.

I had been pulling for a New Zealand boat to win the Cup since the Louis Vuitton challenger elimination races began in April—not easy for a journalist who prides himself on unbiased reportage to admit. The reason I was partial to the Kiwis dates back to 1987, in Fremantle, Australia, when some toad from the *Stars & Stripes* syndicate banned me from its compound.

"You are not qualified to receive press credentials," the form letter read in part—which was certainly true in terms of my sailing background, but I was a fellow countryman, for God's sake, and had traveled 12,000 miles to write about Dennis Conner's bid to retake the Cup. I was not the only journalist, and certainly not the only American, to be brushed off by Conner's people.

The night after receiving that letter, I was roaming around Fremantle when I happened to meet a couple of crewmen from Chris Dickson's New Zealand team, and within an hour I was neither friendless nor storyless. The New Zealanders had a house not far from the *Stars & Stripes* pen—KASA KIWI, a sign over the porch read—and it became my base of operations. The place had two bathtubs, both filled with beer, and plenty of floor space if one was inclined to sleep. The Kiwis shared my outrage: "Conner's bastards won't even let Randy in the door. An American!"

The New Zealanders were full of fun but smart as hell, and brilliant sailors. Yet pulling for New Zealand, I had learned over the years, was like signing on for some accursed hell cruise. In '87, Dickson's *Plastic Fantastic* went 38-1 through the semifinals, only to be shocked, 4-1, by Conner in the Louis Vuitton finals.

In the challenge of '88, Michael Fay tried to manipulate a Cup win through the courts—but was outfoxed by Conner, who used a 60-foot catamaran to humiliate Fay's 123-foot monohull. In 1992, New Zealand was within one victory of being the America's Cup challenger but lost four straight to Italy's *Il Moro di Venezia*. New Zealand's sailors always dominated early and then folded quietly once the withering eye of the world was upon them. It was as if these descendants of sheepherders secretly feared that the jet-set world of international yachting was above their social station and that the back-stabbing, high-tech spook business of the America's Cup was beyond the purview of their small, green nation. Losing was the polite thing to do.

This year, true to form, the Kiwis were unbeatable in the preliminaries. Peter Blake's Team New Zealand was officially 39-3 on the challengers' course but had actually lost only one race on the water. So it was to be Blake's *Black Magic* against New Zealand's old nemeses, Dennis Conner and helmsman Paul Cayard—both of whom in previous years had beaten the Kiwis like cheap rental cars when the chips were really down. In yachting circles, some people believed that New Zealand labored under the dark cloud of its own Cup history: the Curse of the Sheepherders.

So the question wasn't whether New Zealand would self-destruct, but how, and when.

If I had gone to Auckland to watch the races, I could have found out how the locals steeled themselves against the implications of another loss. More interesting, I might have found out why New Zealand was hell-bent on, even obsessed with, winning the America's

Cup. Had any of these people stared long and hard at that 144-year-old trophy? The Cup is one of those rare icons that, like the Hope Diamond, sparkles prettily but implies a dark and sometimes vicious past. In 1851, the hundred-foot schooner *America* won the trophy from the Royal Yacht Squadron of Great Britain, and for the next 132 years the triumphant New York Yacht Club retained it by backing boats that reflected the monetary and technological superiority of the United States—and when all else failed, by hedging the rules. Men such as J. P. Morgan and Harold Vanderbilt saw to that.

The America's Cup trophy is twenty-seven inches tall and looks like a cream pitcher mounted atop a bulb of cauliflower, with facets that are polished to a diamond luster. The facets are a résumé of light, reflecting the blue of open ocean, the pewter of steel mills, the lambency of laser beams, and the silver flash of hard coin—a whole retrospective on what the trophy once was and on the industry that it has come to represent.

Why would pretty, pastoral New Zealand want that?

"In this sport, no one gives anybody a chance, ever." Peter Blake told me that in San Diego, implying that he and his crew of fifteen, plus Team New Zealand's support group of more than forty, had their game faces on, that they were approaching the best-of-nine Cup races with a rugby-tough, kill-the-sick-and-eat-the-weak attitude. No more Curse of the Sheepherders.

The Kiwis won the first race by two minutes and forty-five seconds—the nautical equivalent of blowing the doors off Team Dennis Conner. Even so, Blake was playing it cool, as was the crew. After the race, at the New Zealand compound, the team spent more than two hours washing down the sleek black boat and storing sails, while Kiwi supporters waited beside garbage cans packed with iced Steinlager. It was like a family gathering. The staff was unfailingly gracious, displaying a 1950s conviviality. Everyone wore buckskin-yellow team jerseys ("baby-shit brown," Ken McLeod of Auckland corrected me) and the lucky red socks that had been sold as a fund-raising device but had now become a national talisman.

Though the mood was buoyant, there would be no celebration.

"There's no point in showing any emotion," said David Alan-Williams, who, along with principals Doug Peterson, Tom Schnack-enberg, and Laurie Davidson, helped with the design and construction of the boat that would become known as the fastest in Cup history, *Black Magic*. "There are people who are waiting for the wheels to fall off. We know that. So the only win worth celebrating is the fifth win."

But that didn't stop everyone else in San Diego from having fun—which is why I decided to go there. Not that I couldn't have effectively covered the races via television. Like small wars and manned space flights, a regatta is best understood when bounced from a satellite and filtered through a production room. But the America's Cup is an event, not just a regatta, and a couple of weeks on Shelter Island, the vortex of Cup infrastructure, was just too attractive to pass up. The San Diego Yacht Club, a singularly friendly, unstuffy association, had done a great job of ensuring that the event would be accessible to the world but also have a communal feel. It was a short walk from the yacht club down Shelter Island Drive, past the America's Cup outdoor viewing center, the media hangout at Fiddler's Green, and the Team New Zealand compound, to San Diego Bay, where you could watch *Black Magic* and Team Dennis Conner being towed out to the racecourse.

Few San Diegans did. They were too busy hang-gliding, surfing, playing volleyball, hitting the beaches of Coronado, cruising Point Loma, listening to flawless psych-up music on K-Best 95 radio. Who could blame them? Hell, by the third race, I was doing the same thing.

But the indifference to Cup XXIX wasn't only a California phenomenon. It was a national phenomenon. America's beautiful vision of the America's Cup originated with ESPN's coverage of the Fremantle races in '87 and was expanded in '92 and '95. There were Boat Cam, Pit Cam, Water Cam (until a diver drifted out onto the racecourse and was nearly beheaded), and onboard microphones. People who cared nothing about sailing could hear the dinosaur groans of two sailboats that were as pretty and delicate as damselflies, while great commentary by people like Gary Jobson helped them understand the dogfight they were seeing. The bleary-eyed occupants of 2.4 million homes stayed up to watch the Fremantle races. In '92, the series drew an average of 841,000 homes. But in '95, ESPN's coverage was watched in only 523,000 households.

Why the decline? Among San Diego's nonsailing community, at least, the consensus was that people were disgusted with the endless legal bickering and backroom shenanigans they had come to associate with the event. In the Citizen's Cup semifinals, *Mighty Mary* and Bill Koch's mostly women team ostensibly eliminated *Stars & Stripes* in a much ballyhooed winner-take-all race. In fact, the race meant nothing, because of a twelfth-hour deal struck among Koch, Conner, and John Marshall, president of Pact 95's *Young America,* that allowed all three boats into the finals. When Conner shocked everyone by winning the right to defend, he stirred further outrage by abandoning his own boat and renting the faster *Young America* for a reported amount of $10,000 a day.

To many people with whom I spoke, this was all perceived as sordid business, a kind of sophisticated cheating. In the United States, it deflated interest as certainly as it magnified interest in New Zealand, where more than 80 percent of the households watched the coverage and where people on the streets of Auckland were wearing T-shirts that read, NEW ZEALAND RULES THE WAVES/DENNIS WAIVES THE RULES.

In actuality, the San Diego Yacht Club produced the most equitable regatta in America's Cup history. "Country of origin" limitations were dropped, which allowed all challengers to buy American-made sails, spare parts, and instrumentation. Defenders and challengers had to declare their choice of boats on the same day (in '92, the defense had a six-month advantage) and had to unveil their keels simultaneously.

Even so, Conner became the easy target of all the venom that the controversies had aroused. Journalists are predatory by instinct, and nothing puts blood in the water faster than an overachiever prone to public floundering. And Conner, like anyone who leaves his belly bare while reaching for the top, had done his share of floundering.

On the streets and in the media center, he was slandered daily ("Someone should drive a stake through the guy's heart!" I actually heard someone say), though the source of anger seemed to have less to do with past sins than with the fact that Conner was defending the Cup. A paunchy, middle-aged white male was so . . . un-nineties. *Mighty Mary* was Yoplait; Dennis Connor was Cadillac, for God's sake. Never mind that Conner and his team, in a slower boat, had outsailed the other crews when the real bell sounded.

After being banned from the compound in '87, I was no fan of Conner, but the vitriol that his name evoked seemed unreasonable. As Billy Trenkle, who has worked and sailed for Conner since '83, told me, "Anybody who stands out is going to take some shots, and nobody in the world of sailing stands out like D.C. He doesn't spend a lot of time kissing up, worrying about what the press is saying about him. Which is maybe why the guy you read about is nothing at all like the guy I know. There's nobody I've ever met who works harder at winning, but Dennis is also a genuinely nice man to sail with."

Nice or not, Conner didn't waive any rules when he switched boats. Previous defenders had done things far more outrageous than that. As Pact 95's John Marshall told Peter Blake, "You keep expecting this thing to be fair. The America's Cup has never been fair."

Black Magic just kept winning, putting up extraordinary numbers, leaving Team Dennis Conner so far behind that on occasion the boats seemed to occupy different time zones. Blake and members of his crew had dominated the 1990 Whitbread Round the World Race and in early 1994 shattered records by circling the globe in seventy-six days.

The Kiwis were on a roll, and their black boat really did behave magically. It did what no sailboat is supposed to do: It seemed to ingest the wind, venting the exhaust in a way that created the illusion of jet propulsion.

Even so, Blake and his crew remained stoic. He said things like, "It would be silly to anticipate winning, because we still have a long way to go." Which was true, especially in light of New Zealand's previous campaigns. It was the kind of thing a man says to appease a curse.

But after the fourth race, Peter Blake did allow his expectations to show—just a little. He told a New Zealand broadcaster, "If we are fortunate enough to win, we're going to clean up the Cup rules. Make the regatta ready-steady-even. Same rules for challengers and defenders. If that's to our detriment when we defend, so be it."

He also allowed himself to project what it might be like to host the America's Cup and, perhaps, in so doing opened a small window on New Zealand's long struggle to win. "If we genuinely want to invite the world to come to New Zealand, then we have loads of preparatory work to do back home," he said. "And if we want America's industry to come to us every three or four years, then we'll have to approach our defense in a united way, the same way we approached this regatta. We can't be at each other's throats, like the Aussie defense or like the Americans."

That some American defenders were motivated by acrimony,

not nationalism, was demonstrated on the day of the fifth race, when members of *Mighty Mary*'s crew wore red socks in support of the Kiwis—a brattish stunt that, if pulled by Conner, would have made national headlines.

Black Magic blew the doors off *Young America* a final time and then was towed back to the San Diego Yacht Club to claim the Cup. Immediately, a crowd began to assemble outside the New Zealand compound—dozens of people, then hundreds of people, mostly strangers, all pushing and shoving, trying to get in on the party. The wife of a Kiwi team member was crying—she'd been elbowed. Crewmen at the back of the throng couldn't thread their way to the front. It became a scary scene. The mob just kept pressing forward, while staff members seemed genuinely taken aback that their polite admonitions were ignored: "Couldn't you just back up, please? Please?"

Winning the America's Cup was an invitation to the world, and all that the world implied. Peter Blake had said as much. It took me a while to fight my way out of the compound, but I finally did, and I left wondering: Why would New Zealand want that?

Let There Be Light

I WAS SURPRISED IT WASN'T EASIER TO CONVINCE my old friend Elston that if he joined me in purchasing night-vision goggles, not only would his own pathetic existence be considerably revitalized, but he could also assist me in pioneering traditionally dark venues and revolutionizing outdoor recreation, not to mention the quality of American life as we know it.

"Too much money," Elston said. "If I want to see at night, there's a thing called a flashlight."

I found his attitude disappointing. I had known Elston since high school, and he was never one to shy from experimentation. Indeed, it was precisely because of his love of experimentation that, in the freaky days of the early seventies, we embarked on different paths. I chose a wholesome, productive life and went to work. He chose a beat-up Volkswagen Microbus and went to Berkeley. I'm not going to sit here and accuse an old friend of living in communes and collaborating with hippie scum—although I suspect that's just what Elston did. Nor am I going to accuse him of ingesting many dangerous and illegal chemicals—although, even now, his eyes narrow if an Advil bottle so much as rattles in the next room.

I won't accuse him of any of these things, because an unfair God has allowed Elston—along with many of his counterculture accomplices—to become a respected member of his community, a man of property and portfolios and serious administrative perks. Elston lives in an exclusive Florida yacht club enclave. He leases his vehicles. He attends functions.

I had the catalog open, showing him the goods. "Night-vision capabilities," I told him. "We've been waiting for this all our lives. They sell binoculars, monoculars, high-resolution weapon scopes. They've even got border-guard field glasses."

But I was most interested in the MPN 35K night-vision goggles with the infrared illuminators, the ones once used by Soviet tank commanders. "Easy hands-free operation," I told Elston. "A superb night optics system. Strap them on your face and night becomes day." Because I thought it might awaken his old pinko sympathies, I added, "All this stuff is imported from Russia. Approved by the politburo."

Elston spent a few minutes scanning the catalog before saying, "Those poor bastards. Their marketing instincts are even worse than yours." He tossed the catalog aside and said, "I'm in the mood for some Ben & Jerry's. Have you tried the new Cappuccino Chocolate Chunk? People love it."

I felt like slapping the man. "Gad!" I said. "I'm trying to help you here. Expand your consciousness. With a pair of night-vision goggles we could . . . we could do things we've never done before."

"Yeah?" Elston said. "Like what?"

I cast about for just the right approach, discarding perfectly reasonable activities like viewing nocturnal wildlife, spying on neighbors, turning out the lights and scaring the hell out of party guests.

Finally, I settled on a scenario that was guaranteed to provide maximum leverage. I said, "We can go out in the boat at night and sight-cast to fish."

Elston was an enthusiastic and gifted flats fisherman, and I could see that I had struck a chord. "Fly-fish at night?"

"Exactly. I've never heard of anyone who's tried it. Not with night-vision goggles. As a professional outdoorsman, I feel it's my duty to blaze the trail."

"You know," he said, mulling it over, "most of your ideas are idiotic—but this one has potential." The coast of southern Florida, he noted, had become one big floating zoo. "Every time I go out," he said, "some yahoo runs across my fish, or there's already somebody on my spot. It seems like every yuppie in the world has bought a fly rod and a flats boat."

"But at night," I said, "we'd have the bays and the creeks all to ourselves. Most of those guys are afraid to go out at night. Plus, isn't that when you people attend functions? All we have to do is strap the goggles on and, presto, we'll be able to see tarpon rolling. Or take them to your ranch in Montana and sight-cast to trout."

In a more businesslike tone, I added, "When you think about the hours a night-vision system will add to your recreational day, it's a damn good investment. Very sound."

Elston was making a gesture of dismissal. "Would you quit worrying about money?" he said. "I'll just put it all on the platinum card."

As it turned out, some of my plans for the night-vision goggles weren't exactly revolutionary. Kimberly Johnson, vice president of marketing for Moonlight Products, the country's largest importer of Russian optics, broke the bad news to me. "People have used them for all kinds of things," she told me from her San Diego office. "Bird-watching, camping, night hiking. Since Russia started producing affordable night-vision systems, they've become extremely popular." But then Johnson wanted to know: "Why did you think people bought them?"

I told her that I had the vague impression that they were used by militia groups and goofy paramilitary types.

"No," she replied. "A lot of people buy them so they can keep an eye on their property at night. But mostly they buy them for recreational use." She said her customers have used tanker goggles for cross-country skiing and mountain biking, among many other sports.

"How about for scaring the hell out of party guests?" I asked.

"Probably—they're pretty popular with the Hollywood types."

Damn, I thought, and then offered up my fishing idea.

Johnson seemed confused. "The optics systems can't see through water," she said. "Not unless it's clear. Don't fish live in deep water?"

It was the typical response of someone who has spent too many years in California. I explained to her that, in tropical littoral areas known as flats, big gamefish, such as tarpon, often moved into shallow water to feed. It was not unusual to catch hundred-pound fish in water that was less than four feet deep.

"In that case," she said, "you should be able to see the fish at night, too. It's just such an unusual idea. I've never heard of anyone doing that before."

It was also Johnson who gave me a brief tutorial on how the goggles work. You don't really look through a night-vision scope, she told me. Instead, what you see is an electronic image on a phosphor screen. At night, an image intensifier draws in all available light (stars, moon, streetlights) and amplifies it thousands of times.

The first night-vision devices, she explained, were developed for snipers during World War II. They were "active" systems that required an infrared illuminator and a detector that converted the infrared light into an image visible to the human eye. It was during the Cold War years that the U.S. military developed passive light-amplification systems. Today, the United States is still the leader in night-vision technology, but the third-generation American systems are expensive—anywhere from $3,000 to $15,000. So it is Russia, with its cheap labor and capitalism-happy ex-commie exporters, that has finally made night-vision technology affordable. The MPN 35K tanker goggles sell for only $999 a pair.

Johnson told me a lot of other stuff, too, using words like "photo cathode" and "microchannel plate" that meant nothing to me. But I had all the information I needed. I was going to be the first to use night-vision goggles to fish for tarpon. I was going to revolutionize my sport. America was waiting.

The first thing Elston did when our goggles arrived was pull the blinds and turn out the lights. As I hastened to get my face mask adjusted, I could hear him padding around in the darkness. His cook, Laurita—the poor lady—was with us at the time, and I listened to her speak in a nervous, pleading tone: "Is that you, Mr. Elston? I can't see . . . anything. You're scaring me, Mr. Elston!"

I heard a wicked little laugh, and then moments later I felt a hairy hand grab my shoulder. "Boo!"

I elbowed Elston's hand away. "You idiot! You almost made me swallow my gum!"

"Wow!" Elston said. "What a rush! I can see your aura, man!"

I was fighting to get my goggles on, but somehow I'd gotten the straps all wrong. "Knock it off, Elston. You're starting to scare Laurita."

I heard Laurita's voice: "Why is he acting so strange, Mr. Randy? Please, may I turn on a light?"

I finally got my own goggles in place. I hit the power switch and flipped the binocular caps off, and the room was instantly illuminated. It was like viewing the world through a psychedelic tunnel bathed in a jade-bright glitter. Hit the infrared switch, and a powerful beam swept back and forth with the turreting of my head. The walls of the kitchen seemed oddly bent and slightly out of focus. But I could see Elston plainly enough, looking like some spooky cyborg. Laurita was across the room, her back pressed against the counter. Her eyes were Polaroid white, and her lips were pulled back in a terrible grimace.

I said, "Laurita? Here's some advice. One: Grab a skillet. Two: Don't swing unless you're sure it's Elston."

Several nights later, when we were out in his high-tech flats skiff, goggles in place, Elston said, "Sight-casting to tarpon—this'll be easy!"

It wasn't. Not at first, anyway. We couldn't seem to get the things focused properly. Turned out there were four focus adjustments, not two, as I had assumed. It also turned out that there was a slide device for adjusting the distance between the eyepieces to match the width of the user's face. All of this was key to the user's enjoyment—particularly when the user was being rocketed at forty miles per hour through twisting creeks in the middle of the night.

One thing I didn't like about the goggles was the way they reacted to an unexpected burst of channel-marker lights or even to house lights on the mainland; to each incandescent bulb the goggles added the illusion of a streaking meteor's tail, a fiery arc that shocked the eye.

Once, when Elston noticed me clawing at my face in an effort to get the damn goggles off, he said soothingly, "Hey! Just ride it out. Be mellow. I've been through this hundreds of times. Don't panic—that's the main thing."

Yes, Elston was right at home in that hellish world of starbursts and swirls. Even so, our first two attempts at fishing with the goggles were complete busts. Worse, we were nearly killed when a cruiser came speeding down on our lightless boat. I had to shove Elston from the controls and run the skiff onto a sandbar—a brilliant maneuver that, typically, he did not understand or appreciate. I had to explain to him: "Just because we can see them doesn't mean they can see us, you nimrod!"

By our third trip, however, I was beginning to feel comfortable. It was a moonless night with bright stars. As Elston steered, I sat with the goggles in my lap, looking at the charcoal hedge of islands and the void beyond. Then I put the mask on: The islands became distinct entities with individual mangrove trees; the void became a bright expanse of water and unlighted channel markers. On one of the islands, I watched raccoons foraging. On another, I saw a colony of roosting frigate birds.

Elston ran us within fifty yards of a school of tarpon and then poled us closer while I waited on the bow with my rod. I heard the fish before I saw them—tarpon often make a hushed gulping sound when they breach the surface. Then I could see the fish plainly: chrome-bright animals with wild, horse-size eyes, everything hazed in green light.

It was an extraordinary experience, all the stranger because Elston had brought along a tiny laser pointer that presumably he used at board meetings. Without the goggles, the beam was invisible. With the goggles, though, the laser became a pencil-thin conduit that was perfect for targeting individual fish.

"Isn't this great?" he kept whispering. "You want to talk about mind expansion? This is mind expansion."

It was certainly weird. As the fish moved through the shallow water, they created sparkling wakes of bioluminescence. The goggles magnified the glitter, so casting to the tarpon was like casting to fish that lived among the stars.

I felt a nudge and saw a gigantic, nebulous swirl. I pivoted hard, feeling the gathering weight and velocity of an unseen fish. Then I was watching a four-foot-long tarpon tail-walking away from the boat, slinging water that was a molten gold. As the fish ran, I yelled to Elston, "Didn't I tell you? Things will never be the same again!"

Elston hooted. Then I heard him say, "Revolution, man!"

EMBRACED BY THE
STRANGLER FIG

—————•◦•—————

AFTER SURVIVING A HIDEOUS CAR CRASH in 1980, my friend Tucker Comstock experienced a spiritual refurbishment that helped her shed society's mean limitations and jettisoned her free into a life filled with astonishments of her own choosing—a transcendent journey that would be easier to appreciate if she didn't insist on dragging the rest of us along with her.

"Gad!" I once told her. "The world was a much safer place when you were confined to a wheelchair."

"Quit whining," she replied. "Remember: The world was also a hell of a lot more boring."

It is a point that her friends won't argue. Tucker Comstock can tolerate anything but boredom. Preserved within her is a loony sanctuary of inexhaustible expectation. If something interesting hasn't happened by noon, she jumps into her Land Cruiser and goes looking for it. Any activity, no matter how ridiculous, is preferable to inaction.

Yet even I was surprised when, not long ago, she called and invited me to climb a tree with her in a Costa Rican rain forest. "Don't say no until I've told you about it," she demanded. "This is an amazing tree. It's a hollowed out strangler fig way back in the rain forest. You climb up on the inside—seventy, eighty feet up. You know the best thing? There are bats in it."

Only Tucker Comstock would consider bats an attribute.

Tucker is fifty-one years old. She is five and a half feet tall and weighs 180 pounds. She has hair like Mary Travers and a nose like Joe Palooka. Because of the car crash (she swerved to miss a dog and hit a bridge), her right ankle and her right wrist are fused. Her balance is bad, and her mobility is limited. By her own description, the injuries cause her to walk like a bear.

Before the crash, Tucker says, her life was a mirror of the conventional. She was a good mother, a good wife, a good suburbanite. But after the crash—after months in the hospital, after years in a wheelchair—things changed. Then there was a divorce, and things changed even more.

Many people wilt when their lives have been gutted. Tucker refused to wilt. She was depressed for a time, she admits, but depression was boring, so instead she began to grow. "I've been given a second life," she says. "In my first life, I tried to do everything that was expected of me. Now, in my second life, I try to do everything that's not expected of me."

Tucker runs a small tour company, called Serendipity Adventures, that caters to people who have average or limited physical ability and little previous outdoor experience. She also pilots hot-air balloons and runs her own balloon manufacturing outfit—when she's not paddling white-water rivers, rock climbing, scuba diving, caving, rappelling, or doing just about anything else that will bust her free of the conventional.

"That's one of the reasons I fell in love with Costa Rica," she says. "There are too many lawyers in the United States. People are afraid to try anything difficult, because they might get sued. No more swimming in deserted quarries, no more racing modified cars or renting fast horses. Our legal system has bled away our love of adventure."

Tucker, who is from Ann Arbor, Michigan, first visited Costa Rica in 1989. She says the country was key to her own emotional awakening. Now she has a house there, from which she runs Serendipity. "My legal residence is still Ann Arbor," says Tucker, "but Costa Rica is where I keep my heart."

I was in Costa Rica recently, staying in Santa Ana, a little village near San José, in a house that had a linoleum floor and a television on rollers. Every windowed vista was an illustration of November in a midwestern industrial town. I'd wake up to the sound of cold rain, and I'd go to bed to the sound of cold rain. I endured this only because I was attending a language school, trying to improve my terrible Spanish.

Then, one afternoon, the phone rang. It was Tucker, with her invitation.

The tree, she explained, was located in the northern part of the country, up by the Nicaraguan border. "I figure we'll climb it, then maybe rappel down," she said. "I'm not sure. This is an exploratory climb. If you can make it, the tree might be a reasonable thing for my clients to try." Her friends say that Serendipity is an excuse for Tucker to do the things she wants to do, while providing her with a ready source of unsuspecting adventure partners.

"In other words," I replied, "you want to use me as a test animal. If I can make it, anyone can make it."

"Precisely," she said.

Climb a tree or climb the walls—never did I enjoy a clearer demarcation of options. Even so, I didn't immediately accept. One does not commit to Tucker Comstock lightly. To commit to Tucker Comstock is to be swept away in a mad current of energy. Several years ago, she invited me to go on a short balloon trip with her—I declined—and later she described to me what it was like to teach ballooning to cosmonauts. "Cosmonauts?" I asked. "Oh," she replied, "I didn't mention that the balloon trip was across Russia?"

I suggested that Tucker and I meet for dinner and talk about the tree climb. But when she and Serendipity guide Fernando Giaccaglia picked me up on a Thursday afternoon in her Land Cruiser, Tucker suggested that I pack an overnight bag—just in case. "Unexpected things can happen," she warned.

And she was right. It would be three days before she would return me to Santa Ana.

"If we came here to climb a tree," I said to Tucker, "why are you inflating the balloon?"

We were in northern Costa Rica, on the grounds of the Tilajari Hotel, a pretty place of exotic fruit trees and wild toucans. The Tilajari is owned by Benny Hamilton, a mutual friend and a former Peace Corps volunteer who came to Costa Rica in 1968 and stayed. It was Hamilton who had found the hollow strangler fig and told Tucker about it.

Tucker was standing by the rattan basket, getting ready to light the twin burners. Seventy feet of balloon envelope was stretched out across the grass like a deflated circus tent. "I want to do an aerial reconnaissance first," Tucker said. "We'll fly over the rain forest at treetop level, then try to land in the canopy of the strangler fig. See what it looks like from the top before we approach it from the bottom."

"Sounds exciting," I said. "You can tell me all about it when you get back."

I wasn't about to endorse Tucker's transparent "aerial reconnaissance" gambit. She had been trying to get me to fly with her for years. I am, to be perfectly frank, afraid of heights, and Tucker has long felt that it is her personal responsibility to help me overcome my fear.

"You'll enjoy it," she said. "We'll see lots and lots of birds."

I could see lots and lots of birds from the recliner near the Tilajari pool. "Why don't we just hike into the woods," I said, "and climb the damn tree?"

"I can't hike," she said. "A couple of weeks ago, I slipped on a rock and broke my tailbone." Middle age seemed to be chipping away at her, one body part at a time—not that it was having much effect. "We'll have to take horses to the tree," she added. "But first, we'll go in the balloon. Sooner or later, you've got to get over this ridiculous fear of yours."

Tucker had the burners roaring, inflating the balloon. "You're flying," she yelled.

"No, I'm not," I yelled back.

"Yes, you are!"

As balloon flights go, it wasn't bad. Mariano Avalos, a twenty-year-old Costa Rican, did the actual flying. (Perhaps to avoid being strangled, Tucker wisely neglected to tell me that he was a pilot trainee until we were safely back on the ground.) We drifted along at 4,000 feet. To the west was massive Arenal, an active volcano. Gray exhaust would occasionally gush from its cone, and a minute later we would hear a muffled rumble. Beneath us, unsuspecting horses, cows, parrots, hawks, chickens, and villagers went about their daily lives. We could hear them—each squawk and cackle and moo and whispered word. It was something I had never realized before: Every sound that we make on earth drifts upward, like campfire smoke.

We didn't get anywhere near the strangler fig. In fact, for a hellish, white-knuckled hour, we floated away from the damn rain forest.

Tucker pretended to be disappointed, but she wasn't. "The uncertainty," she said. "That's what I love about ballooning. Living predictably, that's a trap. You know what I've learned from ballooning? I can do anything I want—it just takes me longer. But first I have to be willing to cut loose and let the wind take me."

A friend once had a T-shirt made for Tucker that read, HELP ME, I'VE STARTED TALKING AND I CAN'T STOP.

Sometimes you want her to stop. Sometimes you don't.

On the day that we planned to climb the strangler fig, Tucker was out someplace ballooning—no one seemed to be certain where—so Fernando and I saddled the horses and left without her.

"Tucker can be late," Fernando said. "Or early. Depends on where she is and how much fun she's having." A thirty-one-year-old Argentinean and former professional triathlete, Fernando looks a good bit like Fabio, but he's a hell of a lot funnier.

It took us an hour of riding to get to the forest and then a half-hour of hiking through the forest to find the tree. Just as Tucker had said, it was an amazing tree. I had seen strangler figs throughout the tropics, and I even had one growing on my property in Florida. But never had I seen a strangler fig like this one.

The strangler fig begins life as a vine in the limbs of a host tree. Its tendrils grow downward, binding, fusing, gradually assuming the shape of—and sometimes killing—the host. This strangler fig was ancient, gigantic. The diameter of its base was more than 150 feet, and it extended at least that high up into the forest canopy. The host tree—a massive ceiba or guayabon, perhaps—had long since died and decomposed. As a result, the strangler fig was hollow inside: an intricate, enclosed scaffolding of wooden tendons and vents that was wider than some caves I have seen.

Fernando had brought what he called his tree-climbing experts, four boys—Justin, Josh, Gerardo, and Lee—who were all between the ages of eleven and fourteen. "These are my monkeys," he said. "Children are born to climb trees."

So was Fernando, judging from the way he gibboned his way upward, narrating as he climbed toward the top: "Oooh, there are ants in here! Many ants . . . and they are trying to eat me! Aggh! Bats! There are bats, too! It is getting very crowded up here!"

I went next, and there were indeed many ants and many bats. Even so, it was a phenomenal experience, like climbing into the neck of a dinosaur. Through the skin of the strangler fig, I could hear the rumble of Arenal and the Neanderthal grunt of howler monkeys. When I was about forty feet up, I stopped and peered out a vent into the forest canopy. It did not seem so high, even for a person who is afraid of heights—not after floating at 4,000 feet in a hot-air balloon. There were bromeliads and birds and orchids growing inches away on the outside of the tree. I was on the inside of something that was alive. When was the last time that I had been inside something that was alive?

The boys climbed next, clear to the top of the chamber, about eighty feet up, and rappelled down the outside.

Fernando was delighted. "I will bring clients here," he said. "In time, those bats will come to like me." No doubt. In time, everyone comes to like Fernando.

Hours later, when we returned to the Tilajari, I found Tucker sitting by the pool, sipping fruit juice. "You stood me up," I told her.

"You're not mad," she said. "You're just thirsty." And she ordered me a beer.

It turned out that she had been doing some climbing herself. That morning, her balloon had lodged in the canopy of a tree more than thirty feet above the ground. It had taken her nearly all day to disentangle the thing and then crawl down to earth. As she told me about it, my empathy was sharpened by the pure re-

lief I felt in having not been with her. "It must have been terrible," I said.

Tucker's expression told me that I still didn't get it. "Are you serious?" she asked. "It was great!"

Top Guns of Tobogganing

———•◆•———

Even though my arenas of expertise are canted toward tropical places, I was not surprised to receive a call last winter asking me to add the weight of my outdoor experience to an entry in the U.S. National Toboggan Championships in Camden, Maine. "I'm trying to put together a crack downhill team," someone named Craig Popelars told me. "Every year, a bunch of old college buddies and I get together and do something unusual. You know, travel someplace, try something we've never tried. It's like a reunion. But we're taking this toboggan race seriously."

I was suspicious. A national championship that was open to any wandering ninny who could afford a sled?

"It sounds almost too good to be true, huh?" said Popelars, a North Carolina publishing-house marketer and sportsman. "Our group has already entered two men's teams and one women's team. And as it turns out, we just may have an open spot on the roster."

Although Popelars was coy with me at first, his motive for calling gradually became apparent. As I listened carefully, I realized that he was counting on my well-known leadership skills to guide him and his cronies over the competitive hump.

"That too," he said quickly, "but I didn't mean the weight of your experience. I just meant your weight. As in, how much do you weigh?"

When I told him, he said, "Boy oh boy, that spot is yours if you want it."

Frankly, the guy impressed me. To have one's athletic ability assessed instantly and accurately over the phone is a rare thing indeed.

I tried to picture it: Rent a fast car in Bangor and practice emergency tactical turns on the black ice of Maine's interstate highways. Wear one of those natty red bibs while feasting on restaurant lobster. Climb aboard a toboggan and rocket down an impossibly steep mountain chute in weather so dangerously cold that prudent locals have to employ the buddy system just to fetch the mail.

I imagined a kind of *Big Chill* interplay: Popelars and his friends, a mix of men and women thrown together in a cozy chateau, their emotions fueled by terrifying sled runs, windchill, past hurts and histories, and lots of vacation beverages.

I made a delicate inquiry about the beverage arrangements. "That's the best thing about the whole trip to Camden," Popelars replied. "We've got a fantastic sponsor: Red Ass Ale. It's a brewery out of Colorado. They're providing us with sleds, T-shirts, hats, and more beer than we could ever possibly drink."

"Whatever they're sending," I told Popelars, "just tell them to double it."

I was going to Camden.

Camden's great toboggan race was started in 1991 with the same tongue-in-cheek spirit that inspired its somewhat redundant name: the U.S. National. "That's just the name we came up with," Ken Bailey, one of the founders, told me. "It was kind of a lark."

In '91, Bailey was Camden's director of parks and recreation. Now he's sports and outdoor editor of the Camden *Herald.* Our meeting was serendipitous. Numbed by the eighty-degree temperature drop from Florida to Maine, I had wandered into the *Herald* office because it looked warm and the door wasn't locked. A laundromat would have served, but karma had different plans. The kindly *Herald* staff allowed me to defrost while I listened to Bailey reminisce.

"The way it got started," he said, "a local fellow, Jack Williams, decided we ought to fix up the city's old toboggan chute. We got the whole thing organized. Once it was back on line, we decided to put on a race for the locals. It was just something to do. But we started checking around and realized that with the exception of a few Olympic-type chutes, we've got the only real toboggan run in the country. So whoever won would be national champion, right? We came up with the impressive name, and everyone thought it would be a fun little event."

The first year, locals set a happy precedent by wearing bizarre costumes and treating the one-day race like some outré family picnic. In February, in Maine, even a bad reason to celebrate is good enough. Not a single person froze, hardly anyone was arrested, and word of the event spread quickly to bordering snowbelt states and other sufferers of cabin fever.

After that, the U.S. National Toboggan Championship didn't grow—it exploded. Competitors flew in, their boards checked like baggage, or they journeyed cross-country in Winnebagos specially decorated with team colors. Their custom-built toboggans were coated with their own special bottom waxes—secret formulas, each and every one.

It was craziness, and everyone involved knew it. Which may be why it seemed so reasonable to start taking the race seriously.

As the race's co-chair Sue Chase observed in the presence of a local reporter, "Take a bunch of grown adults, put them all together on a basic item, and they'll immediately discover a way to cheat."

Well . . . maybe not cheat, but competitors did, and still do, try to gain every small advantage possible. The toboggan was invented nearly 5,000 years ago by American Indians, and its greatest attribute—its simplicity—has always provided, for racers, an age-old challenge: How does one make a very simple, runnerless sled move faster than a bunch of other very simple, runnerless sleds? These are not the Cresta or luge sleds that are used in the Olympics. These are your basic wood-on-wood toboggans, six to nine feet long, eighteen inches wide, with rope railings.

The organizers had to invent a number of different classes of competition. They also had to cap the number of entries at 200 and spread the races out over two days. They added a high-tech electronic timing system and included sideshow activities such as dogsled rides, snow-tubing, and the Chili & Chowder Challenge.

It was just before the Chili & Chowder Challenge (great chowder, terrible chili) that I joined Craig Popelars and the proud members of Team Red Ass for our first formal meeting. There were twelve of us, eight men and four women, all close friends except for me.

"This team has only two rules," Popelars told us. He was standing beside the fire at the lodge where we were staying; all of us were wearing our official team hats. "A lot of us," he said, "are from the South, so it's important to remind you: Do not leave cases of beer outside, because they will freeze. And then they will explode."

By putting the safety of his teammates first, Popelars was already winning my respect. I liked his friends, too, all professional people who had come from a variety of states. I liked the way they pretended to ignore their team captain even though they actually hung on his every word.

And rule number two? "Eat lots and lots of food," Popelars told us. "None of that healthy crap, either. What we want is fat, all we can get. The more weight we can put on those sleds, the faster we'll go. Last year, there was a team called the Big Kahoonas that won this thing, and the rumor is that they trained on nothing but kielbasas and cheese dip. If you have any doubts about nutrition, just eat what Randy eats."

Yes, already my leadership skills were binding us as a unit.

I was further heartened when Popelars added, "Remember, people, we didn't come all the way here to Camden to have fun. We came here to win."

Yet it was impossible not to have fun with these people as my teammates. Their reunion spirit proved to be contagious. If they harbored any deep hurts and dark histories, they were far too busy dancing at local nightspots or "dry-practicing" toboggan starts to share them. For hours, we would sit by the crackling fire, four on a toboggan, experimenting with the most effective methods of linking legs over the shoulders of the next sledder.

Another reason it was impossible not to have fun was Camden itself. Surrounded by blue mountains and clustered in a lovely basin where the Megunticook River meets the Atlantic, this old stronghold of dory fishermen is one of the prettiest towns in America.

I arrived on a Thursday for the weekend event and spent my free day viewing the postcard scenery and chatting with the locals. I didn't detect a hint of the hardheaded Yankee coldness for which the region is widely—and wrongly—known.

On the other hand, the weather provided all the coldness anyone could ever want. The temperature perpetually hovered around zero. The simple process of breathing produced an unpleasant crackling sound far up in the nasal passages, the sound of hundreds of mini-icicles thawing and refreezing and then thawing again.

Not that the locals seemed affected. Unlike the snowbelt citizenry of the Midwest, the people of Maine never brag about windchill factor. They don't seem to pay much attention. It's really, really,

really cold. They're well aware of the problem. But since they can't do anything about it, they'd rather not waste the words.

When I informed a wizened gas station attendant that I, a Floridian, was a member of one of the many toboggan teams in town, he studied the scudding clouds in the gray sky, the falling snow, and then calmly suggested, "Might ought to wear some gloves. It can get cold up there on the mountain."

For the qualifying runs at the Camden Snow Bowl on Saturday morning, I wore nearly every piece of clothing I own—including gloves—yet was nearly anesthetized with cold before I'd finished the long walk past the ski slopes to the toboggan chute. "Just try to think of something warm," suggested Steve Hallman, one of Popelars's buddies from North Carolina. "Anything."

Instead, I chose to concentrate on the wintry Mardi Gras scene that was swirling around me: hundreds of people roaming the snow-field, carrying toboggans, polishing toboggans, waiting in a line that threaded its way up the mountain. Many of the competitors were dressed in odd costumes that illustrated the names of their teams: Gilbert's Gimlets (gigantic, furry-green limes), the Hurdling Curds (milk cows with surgical-glove udders), Bobbitt's Blade (don't ask), Bad Habits (nuns), Sister Act (ditto—nuns everywhere), Kevorkian's Alternative (lots of IV tubes were involved), the Beefy Boys, the Beefy Girls, the Fat Bloated Idiots.

"We should have thought of that," Hallman said. "Wearing costumes."

I considered the name of the beer company sponsoring us. "I've been wearing mine," I said, "since the moment I got out of the car."

Popelars had divided the guys into two four-man teams. Chosen for our athleticism and our superior performance at Friday night's practice trials, Hallman, myself, and Joe Bowbliss and Pete Macaluso, both of New Jersey, referred to ourselves as the A-Team.

Popelars, however, was less delicate. "The fat guys take one sled," he told us. "Normal people use the other."

My concerns about frostbite faded as we neared the loading station of the toboggan chute—an apparatus that, to a novice, looks like a rickety hog trough pointed straight toward hell. To qualify for Sunday's finals, we would have to have a very good run. Our pride was on the line, because earlier we had fallen into an unfortunate shouting match with members of Gilbert's Gimlets and made exceedingly rash promises: "See you in the finals!"

Now it was time to produce.

At the starter's call, "Load up!" I squeezed my boots under the curled prow of the toboggan and sat hunched there while my three teammates laced their legs over me and under me—an awkward position that leaves one feeling responsible for body parts that he doesn't own and vulnerable in body parts that he does.

The fact that I was at the front of the sled was not comforting. Sure, no toboggan in the history of the U.S. National has ever gone careening out of the chute and hit a tree or a car or a nun, but that didn't mean it couldn't happen. And who would absorb most of that horrible impact?

But I had come prepared to survive any catastrophe. "You got your catcher's mask on?" Macaluso asked from somewhere behind me. Damn right I did. A Wilson pro model with steel bars, a nice red one that I trusted more than any air bag designed in Detroit.

As bowman of the sled, I also served as the de facto captain. I nodded to the starter. The four of us leaned forward, leaned back, lunged forward again. Slowly, we started to tip . . . Then we dropped from the trapdoor and hurtled through arctic air, as tree limbs and clouds blurred past. The wooden walls of the chute kept grabbing at loose elbows and knees, and the wind screamed in our ears.

We could hear the crowds howling encouragement as we flew across the electronic finish line and clunked down off the track. We slid freely across a long sheet of ice, slowed by occasional patches of snow. We began to weave and fishtail and then finally tumbled off our sled.

The four of us were immediately on our feet, listening for our time over the public address system: 9.42 seconds. Not great, but it was good enough to get us into the finals—the only Team Red Ass toboggan to make the cut.

The next day we would be humiliated by toboggan pros such as Slab City and the Beefy Boys. The final round, I learned, was no place for an amateur from Florida. Represented were the cream of the tobogganing crop, all downhill aficionados who took their body weight as seriously as they took their sleds.

It was an interesting thing to watch, these huge people wolfing foot-long hot dogs, guarding their delicate toboggans as they waited in line, often pausing to inspect the glass-slick bottoms of their sleds. It was their sport. They worked very hard at it and kept their own counsel when it came to secrets of diet or sled design.

Which is why the best times turned in that day were a full second faster than ours—an incremental improvement that may not sound like much, but in fact represents a major shaving off the tobogganer's clock.

It didn't matter much to us. That night, we sat around the fire sipping the official team beverage while Bowbliss played the guitar and Macaluso read his poetry. I watched as the women combed and braided one another's hair. I watched as their men stared at them with affection.

I watched them all, one by one, wait patiently to present their own version of an old story, and I listened to a lot of laughter. The only chill I felt, big or otherwise, was when someone opened the door to rescue more refreshments. Leave beer outside in Maine, you know, and it'll explode.

CROCO%#@! DUNDEE

—————·•·•·—————

STEVE IRWIN, THE KHAKI-WEARING bloke known to millions of television viewers around the world as the Crocodile Hunter, was at this particular spatial juncture oddly, oddly reluctant to converse. Indeed, the man seemed more than merely guarded; he was behaving like some politico who'd just been caught with his snag in the spago. In days to follow, several of his fellow Australians who are in a good position to know would tell me that Irwin can be standoffish not just because of his croc-size ego, but also because there are certain things about his docos that he just doesn't want publicly known.

By "his docos" they were referring to *The Crocodile Hunter,* a documentary television series that enjoys a cultish following in such far-flung places as Sweden, New Zealand, the UK, and numerous countries in Asia. Here in the United States, *The Crocodile Hunter* is one of the most popular shows on Discovery Communications's Animal Planet, the wildlife cable channel ("all animals, all the time") that's now carried in twenty-four million homes around the country. Cable television, as we've all noticed by now, has been experiencing an explosion of fins, fangs, and fur, and Irwin's show is one of the more memorable, if decidedly kitschy, examples of the genre, with its own growing fan club and a seemingly inexhaustible viewership: On Labor Day, for example, Animal Planet aired what it called a *Crocodile Hunter* marathon—thirteen straight hours of the show.

The Crocodile Hunter is a simple, low-budget outback production that joins sometimes thrilling, sometimes mundane wildlife footage with a constant patter of zany dialogue, the combination of which can be quite amusing—though often unintentionally so. Most important, the show gives off the appearance of bedrock honesty. On the tube, Steve Irwin seems like a regular sort of guy who just happens to inhabit a parched world that's wild and rough and very, very dangerous. As Animal Planet's press release puts it, "Irwin is one person who is completely at home in this untamed land. He is a man without fear. He is master of this wild world."

The view that man is the master of all things wild may seem as outdated and hokey as Edgar Rice Burroughs, but the attractive thing to the show's viewers is that it's all apparently real. Irwin really is a bush-hardened Aussie who runs a reptile park, his wife Terri really is an American new to the ways of the outback, and their encounters with snakes, crocs, dingoes, emus, kangaroos, and wombats all actually occur in the wild. "Except for a few fill-in reference shots, we don't fake or stage anything," Terri Irwin would tell me. "Besides, Steve has such great instincts for finding animals, we've never needed to do that."

Then again, I'm from America, for God's sake. What do I know about crocodiles and wombats? What do I know, for that matter, about Irwin's particular brand of outback lunacy? All I know is that I'm a huge fan of the Land Down Under. In my half-dozen trips there, I've come to love the country and its people for their humor and leather-toughness and fair dinkum honesty.

I'd traveled 10,000 miles just to spend a little time with the Crocodile Hunter—at his and Discovery Communications' invitation.

So why was he avoiding me? Was he just preoccupied with filming the show? To shoot a television documentary, one doesn't have to be a butt-dumb drongo or even dense as a bush country dag. But the exigencies of the TV do occasionally make unmanly and sometimes even prissy demands.

To wit: This gray July day in Australia's midwinter, the Irwins had been imposed upon to caravan seventy kilometers southwest of Brisbane to a remote cattle farm near the one-pub village of Rosevale. They'd made the trip for the purpose of shooting fill-in footage and promos. On the bright side, at least for me, this journey would not require that Steve and Terri "risk their very lives in pursuit of Australia's deadliest creatures," as they put it in their publicity material. No, thank heaven. Not even close. This time their quarry was less exotic. They had come in search of dogs. Nice dogs, too: blue heelers, a durable mix of wild dingo and border collie that is a unique product of Australia.

"Almost everyone in Australia claims to own a pure blue heeler," said John Stainton, producer of *The Crocodile Hunter,* "but when push comes to shove, it's always some kind of bloody off-breed. We had to search all over the place to find people who actually work real blue heelers. We're doing a show on dingoes, and heelers are mentioned . . . so that's why we're here."

"Here" was a cattle farm owned by Benny Ahearn and run by Scott and Vicki Mannion, three kind and hospitable people who had agreed to lend their dogs, horses, cattle, and time to the production. The Mannions live in open ranch country in a simple yellow farmhouse that is incongruously ornate and built on pilings—a "Queenslander on stumps," in Aussie lingo.

It was a pleasant thing to watch Benny and Vicki on horseback herding twenty or so Braford cattle for Stainton's benefit. They knew how to sit a horse, and their two dogs were precise and relentless at manipulating cattle. At Stainton's direction, the riders drove the cattle into a paddock, then out of a paddock. They drove the cattle up a hill, then down a hill. "Bloody brilliant!" said Scott Mannion. He was very proud of his wife, as well he should be.

The Crocodile Hunter, meanwhile, was off exploring a nearby pasture, peering up into the trees. "I can't sit still," he said. "It drives me bloody nuts to be sitting on me bum!"

At thirty-five, there is still something unmistakably adolescent about Irwin's pug-flat face and his long blond surfer's locks. Loud-voiced and wide-eyed, he's a person of frenetic energy, like a boy with attention deficit disorder after a very serious Hershey's binge.

An American producer from Discovery Communications had flown in to be on location, and Irwin seemed anxious to impress her. "What I'd like, mate, is to find her a nice redback or maybe a big brown," he said, meaning a poisonous spider or a poisonous snake, one apparently as effective as the other when it comes to impressing American producers. So Irwin was going from rock to rotting stump and turning them over.

Because Irwin had his arm in a sling, I was tagging along behind, assisting him with the rocks and stumps. According to Stainton, The Crocodile Hunter hurt his shoulder recently when he dove out of a boat onto a turtle.

"Turtle?" I asked.

"Yeah," Stainton said. "He messed up the tendons in his arm so bad that the doctors want him to have reconstructive surgery. But Steve won't do it. He doesn't even seem to feel pain like most people. He's an amazing man."

Probably so. But the main thing I'd noticed about Irwin thus far was that he walked fast whenever I walked slow, and he walked slow whenever I walked fast. I was beginning to get the feeling that he didn't want me around.

When I told him that I was looking forward to the next two or three days we were supposed to spend together, Irwin said, "Well . . . we'll see."

"Oh, that's just the way Steve is," Stainton later explained. "You've got to remember that he feels far more at home in the outback than he does with people. He's like a modern-day Tarzan. He really is. That's why people love the show—he's no glib actor. Steve's real."

Steve Irwin isn't Tarzan. He's Mick Dundee, the character Paul Hogan made famous in the movie *Crocodile Dundee*. At least that's the role that Irwin seems to play in nearly every episode of *The Crocodile Hunter* (just as Terri plays the part of the movie's oft-imperiled American heroine, newspaper reporter Sue Charlton). It's a role Irwin has spent most of his life perfecting. He grew up helping to build and stock his father's crocodile zoo, the Queensland Reptile and Fauna Park, which opened in 1971 near the town of Beerwah on the Sunshine Coast. For Irwin's fifth birthday, his dad gave him a carpet python. By the time he was nine, he'd learned to catch crocodiles in the rivers of North Queensland. After graduating from high school, Irwin says, he "traveled for a while, did a bit of surfing, a little camping in the bush."

Then he started volunteering his services to the Queensland rogue crocodile relocation program. "I spent months at a time out in the bush alone catching the largest reptiles on earth," he says. "I lived off the land, gathered me own tucker. I caught heaps more crocs than anyone else working in the program, something like four or five times what anyone else did. When there was a really dangerous croc, I was the bloke they called. I reckon I was the best there was at it, and I just kept doing it."

Well, maybe. Others associated with the Queensland rogue croc program remember things slightly differently. "It's not true that Steve caught more problem crocs than anyone," says Jeff Miller of the Department of Environment and Heritage. "In fact, he never really played a significant role. Personally I like Steve, but anyone who's met him knows he has a tendency to say things like that."

In 1991, Irwin's folks retired and he took over the management of the Queensland Reptile and Fauna Park for good. That same year, American Terri Raines was vacationing in Australia when she happened to visit the park.

"I was instantly impressed by his knowledge and the way he dealt with the animals," she says. Raines had a passion for animals herself, having worked for three years as a technician at an emergency veterinary hospital in Eugene, Oregon. Raines and Irwin both describe their meeting as "love at first sight," and in 1992 they married. "Steve and I are a really great combination," Terri says now. "He's got great instincts for animals, and I'm very good at promotion."

A year after their wedding, the first *Crocodile Hunter* episode was shot. "I don't think of our show as an Australian show," Terri says. "I see it as a global thing, getting bigger all the time. And not just in terms of spin-offs—books, videos, that sort of thing—but also in terms of educating people about wildlife."

Maybe so, but anyone who's seen *The Crocodile Hunter* can sense right off the bat that the Irwins place a higher premium on entertainment than education—indeed, that's part of the program's goofball appeal. The show generally dispenses with the tried-and-true goals of most wildlife shows—namely, to depict animals unmolested and untrammeled in their natural habitat—and instead tries to create, some might say provoke, human-animal encounters.

We watch Irwin poking into caves, prodding snake holes, scouring billabongs in search of various deadly beasts, often with no other purpose than to see how they'll react—and get it all on camera. Irwin seems to have a knack for blundering into hairy situations from which he then heroically extricates himself, and often with a caveat loudly proclaimed to less experienced viewers: "Under no circumstances should you ever try to do what I'm doing! If this spider that I'm holding were to nail me right now, it would be very, very serious business indeed! Just check out those absolutely HUGE venom glands!"

While hunting for crocs or exploring Australia's dingo fence, Terri's life often seems in peril until Steve rushes to save her. In one vignette, she falls out of a boat at night near a hungry croc. In another, Terri screams as the camera captures Steve sprinting to the rescue. A red-bellied blacksnake has blocked Terri's return to camp. "I'm not going to let you bite my wife!" Steve shouts, attempting to catch the snake, while Terri moans, "Oh, Stephen, he's being very naughty!"

Yeah, yeah, it's cheesy and adolescent, but who cares? These people aren't professional writers or actors; they're real-life naturalists trying to show us Australia as it really is. Right?

I was growing suspicious. I spent three days hanging around Irwin's reptile park, trying unsuccessfully to speak with him and waiting to accompany him on an actual shoot. Rain and poor light were legitimate problems. Something that didn't seem legitimate was Terri Irwin's final explanation. "The reason Steve can't talk to you," she said, "is that we're so busy packing to go north for a long shoot. We'd love you to go—the staff thinks you're great. You're exactly the kind of person who'd do well in the bush. But this is the Discovery Channel's shoot, so we can't invite you."

A flattering dismissal, but also odd, because it was the staff of Discovery Communications that had arranged (and seemed eager) for me to write about the Irwins while assuring me that I'd have open access to their shoot.

A couple days later, I placed calls to several eminent herpetologists to gauge their opinion of Irwin and his work. Grahame Webb, who lives in Australia's Northern Territory, is considered the country's foremost expert on crocodiles. Dr. Webb, who has been studying crocs and fighting for their conservation since 1973, is known internationally for the many scientific papers he has published on reptiles, and he is equally well known for speaking his mind.

Certainly he was speaking his mind the day I called him. "I have nothing at all to do with those two," he told me. "I know of no legitimate biologist or wildlife manager who will. Steve Irwin is not a naturalist. He is a showman. He operates a small reptile zoo for profit. He is at least an occasional fabricator who has taken the ethics of television documentaries to a new low in idiocy. The Irwins not only demean Australia's wildlife, they are actually spreading misinformation that is dangerous to anyone who accepts their show as fact. Anyone who's dealt with crocs knows the difference between how wild crocs behave and how zoo crocs or crocs that have been drugged behave—which is probably why television stations in the Northern Territory will not carry their idiotic show."

Webb's last claim is true. According to news director Paul McLaughlin of Darwin's Channel 8, his station received so many complaints after it first aired *The Crocodile Hunter,* the program manager issued a directive that the station would never again broadcast the show.

What isn't true is Webb's statement that the Irwins are shunned by all of Australia's biologists and wildlife managers. Jeanette Covacevich, curator of vertebrates at the Queensland Museum, with whom Irwin sometimes works, describes him as "courageous and hardworking," adding, "He's not a scientist, formally speaking, but he is a self-taught expert when it comes to reptiles." Chris Banks, head curator of the Melbourne Zoo, is another supporter, calling Irwin "a valued and respected consultant."

Still, many well-placed naturalists and reptile experts I called were even less charitable toward the Irwins than Grahame Webb. Most of the critics tended to focus their ire not on Irwin, the private zoo owner, but on his representation of Australia's wildlife. Among other things, his opponents contend that Irwin contrives much of his footage, using his zoo crocodiles to dramatize "wildlife" encounters and, in one episode, even going so far as to let one of his zoo's boa constrictors (supposedly found while shooting) bite him over and over again until his arm was bloody.

One of Irwin's most articulate critics is Malcolm Douglas of Broome Crocodile Park, in Western Australia. Douglas, who is secretary of Australia's Crocodile Industry Association and who says he has been working for the conservation of crocodiles since 1969, told me, "Everyone in Australia involved with crocs knows the show's a fake. What's infuriating is, Irwin makes the animals look like bloodthirsty monsters—which they aren't. A television reporter in Sydney once went to the trouble to prove that the thing's a fake. He took one of Irwin's shows to an expert and demonstrated how the video was spliced just after Irwin jumps out of a boat at night—to give someone time to hand him a croc to wrestle. One of his zoo crocs."

Douglas added, "The one real wildlife encounter he had on his show was with a feral hog, and you'll never see him do that again because he almost got himself killed. The real tragedy is that the Irwins' show is one more example of Australia's wildlife being used as a circus act. The time has come for people to stop making animals jump through hoops—or to wrestle for their lives—just so someone can make a profit."

Frank Mazzotti, an eminent saltwater croc expert at the University of Florida, concurs. "It's the same old alligator-wrestling mumbo jumbo," Mazzotti says. "It has more to do with a carnival act than nature. I'd compare [the Irwins] to magicians, though that's unfair to magicians. Neither of them wants an outsider backstage when the trick's being done."

When I ran some of this criticism by Irwin, he seemed, for the first time, genuinely eager to talk. The Crocodile Hunter denied that he exploits wildlife for entertainment and insisted that he has never administered drugs to crocodiles before capturing or transporting them, "as there is too much risk of killing or maiming" them. He noted that neither Webb, Douglas, nor Mazzotti has ever met the Irwins, let alone seen how they shoot their documentaries. In particular, he suggested that Webb's and Douglas's antagonism is rooted in the fact that both men support the use of crocodile farms as a conservation tool. Crocodile farms are fairly common though controversial commercial enterprises in Australia, and the Irwins have vehemently—and very publicly—fought against them.

"Webb and Douglas absolutely hate us because we oppose their conservation philosophies," said Irwin. "It's ironic that they accuse us of running our park for profit. We don't wake up in the morning with the aim of slaughtering crocodiles for their meat, skin, and by-products. Webb and Douglas are trying to convert saltwater crocodiles into farm-bred handbags."

To Mazzotti's charge that Irwin uses magic tricks to shoot his footage, Irwin replied, "There's no mystery to what I do. I was born in the bush. I've been catching crocodiles since I was a small boy. My training has enabled me to work with potentially dangerous animals so closely it looks unbelievable. It must be very frustrating for my critics to see me at one with crocodiles, knowing they have neither the ability nor the knowledge to work so tightly and efficiently with these remarkable saurians."

Irwin might not like people venturing behind his curtain, but he does emphatically seem to enjoy being on stage. On the day we caravanned to Rosevale, we stopped for fill-in wildlife shots at the Lone Pine Koala Sanctuary, southwest of Brisbane. While we were there, a little boy approached Irwin, tapped him on the leg, and asked, "Are you the man on *Crocodile Hunter*?"

Irwin became instantly animated. Out of the many dozens of people at the park, this little boy was the only one who apparently recognized him. "That's right, mate!" Irwin replied, as if speaking to a crowd. "I'm The Crocodile Hunter!"

"Is that how you hurt your arm?" the boy asked.

"Yep, that's how I hurt me arm! Jumping out of boats onto crocodiles!"

Crocodiles? I thought it was a turtle.

But Irwin was already attracting a crowd with his story. "I jumped out of a boat onto a big croc," he said, "and the croc, he broke all the bones in me arm!"

Bones? Hadn't Stainton said tendons?

It didn't seem to matter much. The Crocodile Hunter was building an audience, and now he repeated himself to inform his new listeners. "Yeah," he said, his voice booming now, "I jumped a big croc—it's what I do, mate!"

Tomato Wars

I DON'T NEED A NEWSPAPER to tell me that life is a predicament. I can look out my back door and suffer the same reminders. Violence, birth, survival, death; throw in dumbness and frustration, too. Out back, I've got a garden. The whole crazy business is right there.

Of late, I have been prosecuting a small war. Hornworms have invaded my tomatoes, and the fighting has been touch and go. They blitz, I raid. I skirmish, they snipe. They are indifferent, I am determined. Maybe the hornworms thought I would stand back meekly and watch. Maybe they just assumed that I was some touchy-feely nineties fop who believed that nature is, naturally, divine and that man, by nature, is an unwelcome outlander, some kind of alien geek.

If so, those little bastards have definitely misread me.

Here's how I discovered the hornworms: I walked out back to do some hoeing and noticed that several of my tomato plants looked as if they had been blasted by a shotgun. That seemed unlikely. Why would anyone want to shoot my garden with a shotgun?

I knelt and saw the hornworms. They were green, nearly as long as my little finger. They had unicorn horns and jaws that resembled old-fashioned ice tongs. At first, I didn't do anything about it. The leaves were actually rather pretty after the hornworms finished with them: lacy and intricate, a kind of snowflake effect. The worms could have the leaves; all I wanted were the tomatoes. Live and let live was my motto. Can you believe I was once so naive?

But then the leaves curled up and the tomatoes scabbed. It was as if the moisture had been sucked out of them. There are few things in gardening more unattractive than a withered green tomato. A withered green tomato looks like illness. A withered green tomato seems to illustrate things unholy.

Many hornworms died unexpectedly that day while being crushed. The battle was joined.

I did something then that I don't normally do: I went to a government office, the local extension agency, and spoke at length with bureaucrats, even though I wasn't threatened with fines or imprisonment if I failed to make an appearance. Isn't it ironic that a garden is supposed to symbolize self-sufficiency but, in fact, forces us into bizarre dependencies?

There I was at the extension agency. There I was waiting in line, reading government bulletins on the wall. There I was asking for free publications, ever mindful that the publications were "provided only to individuals and institutions that function without regard to race, color, sex, or national origin."

Fortunately for me, hornworms were not covered under this caveat. The free pamphlets got right down to the nitty-gritty— namely, how to exterminate the vermin. "There are no reliable non-chemical control measures," one stated, and then went on at length to describe several poisons that would do the job.

For me, that was a problem. Early in the game, I had bragged to several local aficionados that mine would be an organic garden. The declaration hadn't been volunteered. The aficionados had asked, and I had told them what I believed they wanted to hear. Gardeners tend to be very judgmental people. Don't let those sappy smiles fool you. Dodging their disapproval seemed to be an act of kindness to us all.

Also, I liked the idea of eschewing chemicals. I wouldn't have to drive to the hardware store, I wouldn't have to buy one of those spray tanks, and I wouldn't have to wash my hands before popping open a beer. Organic gardening offered dual advantages: It was the politically correct thing to do, plus it was less work. But now I was stuck. If I started pumping my garden full of poison, the aficionados would find out about it. Gardeners are not only judgmental, they are nosy as hell.

"Prior to planting, the wise gardener assembles a plan for effective pest control," one pamphlet read. Obviously, I was not a wise gardener, but I didn't need to be scolded by some government hack. Weren't the hornworms punishment enough?

"For the eco-sensitive organic gardener," read another, "hornworms can be easily removed by hand and released, unhurt, in other areas."

There—my instincts had been right to begin with. Although where was the fun in releasing the worms unhurt? Where was the justice?

I thought about that for a while. Then I got a bucket and took the pamphlet's advice.

Several days later, a nosy gardening aficionado stopped to chat. "How's your garden?" she wanted to know. Fine, I told her. My tomatoes were doing much better.

"Not mine," she replied. "Something terrible's happened. Mine have been invaded, they're an absolute mess. I've never seen so many hornworms in my life!"

As has been true with so many interesting discoveries throughout my life, my discovery of gardening was accidental. I was a twelve-year-old 4-H Club member when the pig I was raising for the fair wandered away from the trough and intersected with a truck. I heard the tires screech and ran out into the twilight to see the driver climbing shakily from his big diesel Peterbilt. "I just hit something!" he called to me. "What'd I just hit?"

My black-and-white Poland China pig was what he had just hit. Whew, some mess.

"Are you sure? You don't have any brothers or sisters?"

I did, but they didn't have black hindquarters and a blunt snout. Nor did they gallop around naked at dusk on a fast country highway.

"Thank the good Lord," said the driver. "It looked just like some chubby kid."

The driver could afford to relax. He didn't have a 4-H project due in the fall.

I spent the next couple of days reviewing my options. No way was I going to enter my Arabian mare again. She cribbed constantly, which made her flatulent, and she bit like a dog. I had spent too much time around horses to have anything but contempt for their deviousness. I didn't have time to raise a steer, and a fox had recently eaten most of my banties. If I caught the fox, maybe I could enter it?

No. 4-H didn't sanction fox husbandry.

I planted a last-minute garden by default, planted it next to my mother's garden, which ensured that it would survive because she was a dedicated gardener and would do most of the work. I grew beans and corn and peas, and I didn't enjoy it at all. About the only thing I learned was never, ever plant anything that has to be snapped or shucked or hulled. Too boring, and way too hard on the fingers. Plant only big stuff, vegetables that come off the vine ready to eat.

Worse, I had to show the results of my garden project at the county fair. Lead a 300-pound Poland China through the midway, and even if people don't respect you, they will behave as if they do. But carry a basket of iceberg lettuce, and the carnies will chatter at you like magpies. While my fellow 4-H members strutted around with their pigs and steers on leashes, I hid in the exhibition building with a bunch of old people who smelled of Milorganite and mothballs. Most of them wore those sappy gardener smiles. Some things never change.

When the 4-H judge got to my exhibit, he hesitated before he said, "I'm curious. What motivated a kid like you to plant a garden?"

"Had to, sir," I told him. "My hog got mashed by a semi."

The judge seemed relieved. Yeah, a dead pig, fancy snow peas. It all made sense.

Decades passed, and I never planted another garden. Didn't feel the slightest urge. Then, a year ago, I happened to eat an unusually good avocado. I had found it on a remote island. Since the chances of getting back to the island were slim, I suspended the avocado seed in a glass of water, and a frail sapling grew out of it.

I took the sapling out back, planted it, and . . . something happened. I'm not sure what. It was as if a door in my brain had creaked open, exposing an unused room, a dusty private place, the gazebo of the mad gardener. The feeling had something to do with getting my hands in dirt; something to do with the roots of the sapling functioning beneath the soil, unseen; something to do with the orderliness of it, of planting a specific tree and receiving a specific fruit in kind.

I became obsessive. I bought the *Old Farmer's Almanac,* I visited garden-supply shops, I spoke with experts. Because I now live in South Florida, there were all kinds of exotic tropical fruits and vegetables I could grow. And because I had traveled through many of the exotic homelands of those fruits and vegetables, growing them would, in a way, reunite me with the places I had been.

I liked that.

I got to work and staked out my garden.

My weekend cabin is located atop a shell mound on an island off Florida's western coast. The garden is laid out behind the cabin in an earthen plaza that archaeologists have informed me was constructed by the indigenous people who built the shell mound. As I hoe and weed the soil, I commonly find pottery shards that could be a thousand years old, maybe older. The indigenous people on this coast were pot makers and pot breakers. The ground is littered. However, they weren't farmers—although the Europeans who arrived later were. I wasn't the first to till the plaza, but I am its current steward. There are times when the weight of tradition weighs heavily on my shoulders.

Back there in neat rows are, among other things, three varieties of pineapples, eleven varieties of bananas, key limes, atamoya, papayas, a whole bunch of herbs, and okra, too. And, of course, tomatoes.

Sound idyllic? That's what most gardeners—particularly the editors of gardening magazines—would have you believe. It's not.

Let's walk down the mound and take an honest look at what is really going on. Ignore the first couple of rows. Those are herbs.

Beyond them, though, are my favorite plants: the hot peppers. I have habaneros, jalapeños, cayennes, naval chiles, eighteen different kinds of peppers in all, grown from seed stock collected around the world. I use the peppers in cooking, I pickle them in vinegar, a neighbor makes a wonderful chutney out of them. It's rare that a visitor doesn't leave with joyful tears in his or her eyes after sampling one of my peppers right off the vine.

So what's the problem? Birds are the problem. Birds have been eating my chiles. They fly down when I'm not looking and then they steal them, simple as that. Before I started a garden, I liked birds. Not anymore. Birds are nothing but thieving scum. I can't say it more plainly. A gardener can only be pushed so far.

You know about the tomatoes, but I've had my problems with the pineapples, too. It's possible, just possible, that they have been infected with mealybugs or red spider mites. To me, the crowns of the plants look a little too yellow to be healthy. It worries me. I fret about it at night. Has that woman with the recent hornworm problem retaliated with the first salvo of what is, in effect, biological warfare?

I wouldn't be surprised. The first symptom of obsession is tunnel vision, and its first casualty is rational thought. Does this woman really believe that her garden is the only one in the world that matters? What an ugly stunt to pull. If she were half the woman she pretends to be, she would confront me man to man. But no, she attacks innocent pineapples instead.

The next two rows are empty. They aren't supposed to be empty, but they are. I planted watermelons there. The watermelons grew up thick and green, then just disappeared. One day they existed, the next day they did not.

Initially, I suspected fire ants. The first axiom of horticulture is that there are way, way too many insects in the world. Fire ants are the worst. They will attack root systems as brutally as they will attack a gardener's bare legs. These little Nazis wait until there are about a thousand on you, and then they all bite at once. Extermination is exactly what they deserve, and I try to do my part. I love the smell of ant poison in the morning.

But fire ants didn't take my watermelons. Possible clues to the truth can be found trailing from the banana patch, right through my peppers: cow tracks. Next door there are cows, and apparently those cows have learned how to open the gate—it's the only explanation that my indifferent neighbor will allow. Every chance they get, his brutes stomp through my garden, splatting their nasty pies.

See? Gardening isn't idyllic. But I keep at it, trying to plant more, trying to learn more from people who are experts in the field.

This isn't easy, either, because expert gardeners aren't exactly social butterflies. Worse, they tend to be political radicals. I don't know why this is true, but it is. Nearby lives an authority on tropical fruits. He is a brilliant man whose years working in Central America and Asia familiarized him with all the exotics I would now like to grow. But his years abroad also left him cold on communism, and sharpened his partisan fears, so conversation with my friend requires a certain delicacy.

"You ever notice," he once said to me, "that Bolshevik rhymes with bullshit? Bolshevik . . . bull-she-it. See?"

"Amazing," I told him. "How insightful! Now about those Persian limes I want to plant . . . "

An expert on organic gardening also lives nearby. Her partisan worries come from a different wing of the same goofy house. "Meat eaters are going to destroy this planet," she once explained. "Do you have any idea how many millions of acres are being laid waste by cows?"

Did I ever. "I don't like cows," I told her. "A cow stole my watermelons."

Yes, she said, but sheep and horses were no better.

"Exactly," I said. "Gad, don't get me started on horses!"

A garden mirrors life, and life is just one damn thing after another. I don't need a newspaper to remind me of that. The mad gardener has escaped from the gazebo; I'm receiving updates daily.

HALF MAN

I'M NO ADMIRER OF TABLOID NEWSPAPERS, but last November, while standing in line at the grocery, I noticed a startling headline on the front page of the *Weekly World News*: "Half-Alligator, Half-Human Found in Florida Swamp!"

Was it possible that such a beast could have been captured without authorities notifying one of the nation's foremost authorities on kindred phenomena—me?

Yes. Apparently; although, even by the tabloid standards of carrion journalism, the claim seemed outrageous. But the accompanying photograph, at least, had to be given serious consideration. The image was terrible to behold: the dehydrated head and chest of a human growing from the body of some kind of crocodile. It had tiny little clawlike hands and a facial expression that might be grotesque by decent standards, but is all too common on Florida's beaches: the Spring Break glaze; a dumb, expectant look, as if the jaw has thawed too quickly beneath two frozen but eager eyeballs. Undeniably, the photograph had the ring of truth.

Even so, as an expert, my initial assessment was that an alligator had swallowed the bottom portion of some unfortunate man. A German tourist, perhaps—the Teutonic life expectancy in Florida is now exceeded by some species of mayfly. Indeed, a German tourist had recently disappeared a few miles from my own southwest Florida home. If a massive manhunt had not finally found him wandering crazed after three hellish nights lost in the mangroves, he, too, might have become part of the food chain; claimed by some bull gator that could not ingest more than half of anything weaned on sauerbraten. It made sense.

But the *Weekly World News* insisted upon another explanation. According to the accompanying story, the creature had been found, alive, by two hunters who wanted to kill it. Fortunately for the creature, a paleontologist, Dr. Simon Shute, happened to working on a nearby Indian mound, and he, along with a Florida bureaucrat, interceded. After saving the creature, Dr. Shute and the bureaucrat, true to the traditions of their vocations, decided to take responsible action. The creature had presumably been living innocently in the Everglades, wild and free, a threat to no one. Their duty was clear: not only was this thing unregulated and unlegislated, worse, it was also untagged. So they roped the creature, caged it, then transported it to a secret marine lab in the Florida Keys.

"We are now conducting a search for more Gatormen," Dr. Shute was quoted as saying. "There are more out there."

Undoubtedly . . . if the story was true. And granted, some of the *Weekly World News*'s details were compelling, if not convincing. But the whole tale was unraveled by a couple of key points that any sophisticated reader would spot as pure fantasy. One: if a Florida bureaucrat—or any bureaucrat—had truly been involved, he would not have attempted to capture Gatorman alone. He would have used his cellular phone to call for backup. Two: If Gatorman was accurately represented by the photograph, if his physiologic components had not somehow been reversed by a darkroom trick, the *Weekly World News* would not have quoted Dr. Shute. They would have quoted the creature. Unless Gatorman spoke only German, in which case, the tabloid would have invented a quote and used it anyway. Something tart and suitably Germanic, such as: "If I am to be extracted from this animal, let it be through the front exit!"

Obviously, the photograph was there, but the facts were not. It was a fascinating problem—not because I believed Gatorman existed, but because I have a long-standing interest in those strange and weird beasts that inhabit the human mind with far more certainty than they inhabit the regions that are credited with hiding them.

Intentionally or not, I think most outdoors people collect these stories; I have done so to the point of expertise. Indeed, they contribute to a pet theory of mine: The decline of a wilderness region can be gauged by the decline in the number of folklore creatures said to inhabit it. And another: Folklore monsters instantly illustrate the geographical feature a region's human residents most fear.

Naturally, because I live in Florida, I was pleased to read about Gatorman—for the last few years, this state's most feared geographical feature has been Miami; its monster, the feral adolescents who stalk it. A half man, half alligator living in the swamps seemed pristine and reasonable in comparison. Just the rumor of such a thing earned back some respect for the Everglades. And it seemed to kick a little of the starch out of the bureaucrats who now dominate the place.

Over the next few months, I checked out details of the Gatorman story, and discovered the following:

No paleontologist I could find had ever heard of Dr. Simon Shute.

Shute's name does not appear in Florida motor vehicle records, nor in any Florida telephone directory.

No one by the name of Dr. Simon Shute had ever applied for a state or federal grant—final, bedrock proof that the man did not exist.

Half Man

Edward Klontz, editor of the *Weekly World News,* might have a comment on the origin of the Gatorman story, but doesn't return phone calls. (Not mine, anyway.)

The *Weekly World News* is known as Whacky World News to some reporters at its sister paper, *The National Enquirer,* one of whom told me, "Whacky World is a big moneymaker, but you can't believe anything in it." (A searing indictment, considering the source.)

Yet the photograph was real, of that I was convinced. But each refuted detail was like a bullet in Gatorman's breast . . . or maybe his thorax. Hard to say for sure. Anyway, I dropped the investigation . . . until, by coincidence, a Louisiana friend mentioned that he knew a man who knew a man who, many, many years ago, had seen a creature fitting Gatorman's description, alive and on display, at a New Orleans brothel.

I'm I making this up? Nope. Was my Louisiana friend? Nope. Was the long-gone man making it up? Probably.

It didn't matter. America and its wilderness are being urbanized, neuterized, and sanitized on an hourly basis, and those of us who love wild places—and the folklore creatures that are a measure of their vitality—have to be content with what we can get.

My search would continue. Even if it meant going to New Orleans.

HALLOWEEN'S TIMING IS OFF; spring is when the creatures come out. It's the first March thaw that lures to field and wood and bog the hibernants and winter dozers and God only knows what other hellish beasts. I don't say this from rumor or cheap hearsay; I know from early experience. I was just an infant when I had my first encounter with a yeti-like creature—or so my mother told me. We were living in a remote farmhouse in Ohio; my father, a highway patrolman, was away on duty when, one March night, my mother was awakened by the steady thud of someone—or some thing—walking outside. Then the house begin to shake, as if massive shoulders were being rubbed against the clapboard. For nearly an hour, the assault continued. We had no telephone. My mother lay awake until dawn, then went outside to investigate. There had been a fresh snow. Her description of what she saw never varied over thirty years: The prints of a barefooted man circled the house; each print a broom handle and a half apart. Caught in the clapboard were tufts of silver hair. A farmer happened by, and the two of them measured the prints again. The farmer contacted the state patrol, but the snow melted, and the evidence disappeared.

In later years, I would say to her, "It was a cow." She would reply, "Honey, I know cows. I grew up with cows. Don't tell me about cows." I would say, "Then it was a bear." She would reply, "If it was a bear, I'd hate to try and buy shoes for it. The Sears catalogs don't mention size 20 D." Then she would add, in a mildly accusatory way, "And you slept through the whole blame thing."

What did she expect? I was an infant at the time, and not equal to a more mature response. When one is incapable of diving under the bed, one is better off sleeping. It's nature's way.

I believe what my mother said; I don't believe what she saw. Not the way she interpreted it, anyway. But the place where we lived was a desolate, unpeopled place—if not wild, at least isolated enough to empower all the potential of human imagination. That requires space. It requires inaccessible thickets, or swamps, or lakes without bottoms, or murky water, or a wooded place not veined with trails.

North Carolina, where most of my family has lived for generations, had all of the above, plus plenty of aunts, uncles, and cousins to share tales about them. There were the Brown Mountain lights—lights of a ghostly source that we never saw, but we knew plenty of people who had. There was the Devil's Circle, where nothing ever grew, or could grow, because of an ancient curse. For a similar reason, there were the prints of a horse's hoofs at Bath that were indestructible, and there was a creature that inhabited a bog on the Pee Dee River, only some said it was a giant eel. Then there was the pack of wild dogs that roamed the piney woods, grown huge from feeding on solitary fishermen and kids foolish enough to camp in the woods alone—which we often did. I grew up hearing all of this . . . but believing none of it (well, except for the one about those damn dogs). I wish I did. I wish I could.

Even so, I liked the stories. My theory about the relationship between true wilderness and folklore monsters evolved. Which is why I am not surprised that, as the population grows and spreads, the regional creatures are disappearing. They are an endangered species not mentioned on any government list.

Before proceeding with my investigation into Gatorman, I decided to contact a few knowledgeable people around the nation and inquire into the well-being of creatures in other regions. I was lucky enough to reach Allan W. Eckert, author of the six-volume historical series, *Narratives of America*. Eckert, from his home in Bellefontaine, Ohio, described in broad-brush fashion a variety of folklore monsters, including a gigantic black cat that was said to roam Ohio's hill country, and a great wolf of the Plains states that could destroy half a herd of cattle in a night. "I think most of these stories come from a period when people had enough leisure time to sit on their front porches and trade stories," Eckert told me. "Maybe that's one reason I seldom hear them now. When I did hear them, it was usually in the spring, when the weather allowed people to get out, peaking during the summer dog days, when the little newspapers didn't have much other news to publish."

In Nebraska, Joe Arterburn, as a member of Cabela's outfitters staff, converses daily with outdoors people, and I decided he would be a good one to ask. But, like Eckert, he hadn't heard a fresh story for many years. "You used to occasionally hear of a Bigfoot sighting," Arterburn told me. "But not often. It stands to reason because there aren't a lot of places to hide in Nebraska."

I received a similarly disappointing report from writer Lionel Atwill in America's Northeast. "Even Champ, the monster of Lake Champlain, hasn't been reported in a while," he said. "The little town of Port Henry, New York, makes a living off those stories, and you'd think Champ would show a little more concern for their welfare."

The cynosure for reports of unidentified creatures, though, is the International Society of Cryptozoology, located in Tucson, Arizona. According to Society secretary, J. Richard Greenwell, cryptozoology is different from other forms of the discipline in that it not only welcomes anecdotal information about undiscovered species, it seeks them out. "A cryptozoologist becomes interested in a supposed animal based on previous information. Folklore, archaeological artifacts, native accounts, old historical narratives—we use all of these sources. Then we take a hard look at the data and try to decide if the supposed animal really could exist. If we're interested, we make a very deliberate search for the animal. It's a different philosophical approach than regular zoology."

The Cryptozoology Society comprises more than 800 members, according to Greenwell, many of them highly regarded professionals. "We're not in the sensationalism business," Greenwell told me. "Indeed, we avoid it. We try to go about the business of investigating previously unidentified species in a very careful way, and publish the results of field workers in our quarterly journal (an annual membership in the Society is $30). We try to assume nothing, then assign a percentage of probability. The Sasquatch, or yeti, for instance: If it does exist, I find it incredible that, despite hundreds of reported sightings from almost every state, that not one specimen has been shot and killed by a hunter, or hit and killed on the highway or collected in some fashion. Yet we still try to approach the possibility of it existing with an open mind."

Greenwell didn't think much of my folklore-requires-wilderness theory. "No, a whole new mythology has evolved," he said. "Urban folklore. It's like the stories of alligators and turtles living in the sewers of New York City. We've all heard the stories; some believe them. But there was only one verified case of an alligator being found in those sewers, and that was more than eighty years ago."

Nor did Greenwell give much credence to my story about Gatorman. "Years ago, there were a few reports about some kind of swamp creature that fits that description. But we've dismissed them as too bizarre. And the reports came from the Carolinas, not Florida."

My God. Was the bastard following me?

I WENT TO NEW ORLEANS. I ate some great food; did the usual things. But I didn't find Gatorman. Over the phone, Angus Lind, a columnist for the *New Orleans Times/Picayune* told me a wonderful story about the *loup-garou,* a werewolf-like creature said to live out in the bayou. Then I spoke with Joe Rau, a collector of antiques and stories, who said he knew a man who ran a small museum in Long Beach, Washington, who might have all the information I needed.

Rau was right—that's where I found the half man, half alligator as pictured in the *Weekly World News.* Not that I went to Washington. There was no need. Wellington Marsh, owner of Marsh's Free Museum in Long Beach, sent me a postcard of the creature—a creature he has owned, and had on display, for many years.

"I don't know how that newspaper got a hold of my postcard," Marsh told me, "and I don't know why they made up the story to go along with it. I call the thing Jake, and he's very popular with the folks who come through the museum. When they ask me about Jake, I tell them the truth. I don't know if he's real or not. But I know a man who knows a man who said he saw a creature just like Jake down someplace in Texas."

"Texas?"

"East Texas. In some kind of swamp or something. Not that I believe it."

Even so—the search continues!

RUNNING TOURS

MAYBE THROUGH INFLUENCE, but probably through curse, the Temple of the Giant Jaguar was the shaper of my personal policy on urban transportation. I can blame it, thank it, love it, hate it, but the policy remains as unyielding as ever. When I arrive in an unfamiliar city, any city, I lose all control of the itinerary. I store my gear, put two bottles of beer into a bucket of ice, then I go to the streets and run. Damn the cabs, the buses, the rickshaws and yak carts, I run. I run aimlessly, though not without purpose, and it doesn't matter if I am above the tree line or below the equator— which is why I'm pretty certain that I now travel under the effects of a terrible Mayan whammy.

It all started many years ago in the jungles of Guatemala, at the ancient city of Tikal. Located 190 miles north of Guatemala City, Tikal is a massive ruin of temples, shrines, and triumphal platforms. Before the birth of Christ, and up until about 900 A.D., this now silent place was a ceremonial center of the Maya, an astonishing people. Generations of craftsmen, mathematicians, priests, and their progeny lived, thrived, and died here. But now, when approached from the air, the only hints of long-gone human commerce are the bleached roof combs of pyramids that poke through the rain forest canopy.

I had been to Tikal twice in previous years but, on this particular trip, I came by Land Cruiser, not by plane. I was on my own, free to roam haphazardly among the remnants of eleven hundred years of ceaseless construction. There were tour groups in the park—there always are—but I held my ground, for I had decided to select one small piece of Tikal, and spend the whole day there. When I say "piece" I mean just that. There are six square miles of ruins, and it is numbing if one tries to see too much. The etched stonework soon blurs. Also, a Zen Buddhist friend had recently implied that I lacked spirituality—a ridiculous charge. Even so, I thought that by enduring several boring hours meditating over a single carving, I could prove to this curd-eater that I was as spiritual as the next guy.

The area I chose was the Great Plaza, where the Temple of the Giant Jaguar faces the Temple of the Masks. Lying between is a lawn running east and west, on which are several stelae—carved stone markers—and it should have been easy to select an etching, then to sit in quiet communion with the brilliant Maya of long past.

But it wasn't easy. Tour groups kept queuing up, talking loud. And the strolling beer salesmen wouldn't leave me alone. Stare as I would at the bizarre mosaics of animals with human heads, human bodies with jaguar faces, the weird feather-work on snakes, fish and other strange creatures, I just couldn't concentrate. As reckoned by the Mayan calendar, I sat there for less than One Kin—in American time, the equivalent of about a six-pack. But daylight is not conducive to meditation; sitting quietly just invited interruption. And walking wasn't any better. I tried it. Which is when I made a fateful decision: I would return to the Temple of the Giant Jaguar that night and have the whole place to myself.

I should say right here that it is illegal to visit the pyramids after dark. Not only that, it is dangerous. As Carlos Ortiz, manager of the nearby Jungle Lodge, explained to me, an armed guard with a dog patrols the park grounds once the gates are locked. Not that I told Ortiz of my plans. This nice man wouldn't have allowed such lunacy. But I was determined to do it, and I did.

I left the Jungle Lodge at about 11 P.M., carrying only a Mini-Mag flashlight, though I did not use it to find my way. No. I didn't want to alert anyone. Above, there was no moon, but stars eddied in a black vacuum, which was light enough. It is about a mile from the lodge to the Great Plaza, and I took my time, walking slowly. I found the fence, climbed it, then felt my way along the earthen path that tunneled through the trees. There is a density to the rain forest at night. The weight of it descends, and it is a little like walking under water. It was quiet, too; a crackling, whirring kind of quiet, like the sea bottom at two atmospheres, and I had to remind myself to breathe. But, soon, the tree canopy thinned. Stars reappeared. And then the Temple of the Giant Jaguar rose out of the gloom, a pyramid in silhouette against a scrim of deep space.

The Temple of the Giant Jaguar is nearly 150 feet high, and a ramp of stone steps leads to an open chamber at the top. I couldn't wait to get up those steps—not because I was eager to meditate, but because I was worried about the guard and his damn dog. They could have jumped me at any time back in the forest. But, once I got to the top of the pyramid, I'd be safe. What kind of dog would charge up several hundred steps just to bite someone? Certainly not one of those curly tailed curs common in Central America. So I half walked, half crawled up the steps to the top of the pyramid, and took a seat on the stone platform. I was above the tree canopy now. The rain forest of Peten rolled away in charcoal mist, and it was a little like sitting above the clouds. It should have been wonderful. From this distance, the jungle glittered with fireflies—millions of them, detonating randomly. There were so many fireflies that, visually, the effect became disturbing. My ears kept straining to hear the noise of those mini-explosions but, of course, there was only silence; a deep and complete silence, and I began to imagine that I had gone deaf.

I decided to change the mood by exploring inside the pyramid chamber. For the first time, I used my flashlight, shining it on the carved lintel above the middle doorway. After all, this is what I had come to do: ponder the strange etchings of the Maya. This wooden lintel, more than a thousand years old, was an extraordinary artifact. Carved into it were swirling feathers that seemed to form a human face. That figure was connected to an inlay of rectangular shapes that formed more human faces; a complex mosaic, each connected to the other. The longer I looked at it, the more faces appeared. Gazing at these long-dead people, just them and me up there alone in the dark, my true spiritual nature really kicked into gear. Also, it began to get a little spooky. There was a beautiful woman wearing a headdress. Her black eye held me, then dismissed me. And there was a nobleman with something coming out of his ear. A snake? Yes, a snake . . . and the snake seemed to be crawling toward the open mouth of . . . of a with-ered old hag who was . . . Gad! . . . who was copulating with a jaguar.

I backed away from the lintel, filled with a growing sense of fore-boding. During the day, Tikal was as benign as a museum, but now, in darkness, it seemed an eerie reunion place of the ancient domin-ion. And I had the strong feeling that none of those lost souls wanted me there. I found the stairs and began to work my way down, slowly, slowly, because the old hag on the lintel had the fickle look of a prac-tical joker. Tripping would have been fatal, but murder is small po-tatoes to anyone who would mate with an animal. Back on the ground, I began to walk calmly toward the Jungle Lodge. I was no longer worried about the guard. I would have welcomed human company. And if the dog attacked . . . well, the old hag would know how to handle him, the poor bastard. Just thinking about her witchy face goaded me to walk faster . . . faster . . . until, soon, I was jogging . . . jogging because I had the terrible impression that all the grotesqueries of that place were rising up in my wake . . . jogging at a strong, steady pace, to hell with the darkness and the bad footing. Once I kicked a log and fell, but I got right back up and began to jog again. And it was during that fast retreat to the lodge that I had a flash of realization: The instant I had started jogging, the forest ceased to be a weight above me; the ruins of Tikal were no longer a sinister presence behind me. The simple act of running had transformed my relationship with the surroundings. I felt safe in a sphere created by my own exertion, which was a wonderful feeling. I could still smell, hear, and see the forest, but I was doing it on my own terms. Sitting or walking seemed prissy in comparison. Spirituality? I'm still as spiritual as the next guy, which is to say that, if God or His long dead want to communicate with me, they can dial direct, day or night, just so long as they leave that jaguar humper out of the loop. Otherwise, I'll be out there running, emotionally bullet proof.

WHICH IS PRECISELY HOW my personal policy on urban transportation was shaped. An ancient city, an old city, a modern city—I now treat them all the same. As mentioned, the first thing I do upon arrival is store my gear, arrange for refreshments, then pull on shoes and shorts, and go for a run. An hour on the street cuts straight through the tourist brochure malarkey; brings smells, sights, and sounds straight to the senses, no middleman. Tour buses? They're too confining, plus the guide always expects a tip. Same with cabs. A bicycle would be good, but where is one going to get a bicycle? Skates, ditto. And forget those low-impact walking tours—just too much risk of injuring an elderly person.

No, running is the best way to go. Prior to suffering the curse at the Temple of the Giant Jaguar, layovers in cities were sensory vacuums: hotel pools, clock watching, and dull museums. Now layovers pack a punch; little mini-adventures with all kinds of potential. The trick is to go properly prepared, and with the right attitude. Remember, on a running tour, fitness is a peripheral benefit, not an objective. If you pass an interesting monument or shop, person or pub, you are not only allowed to stop, you should stop. Also, never preplan your route. There is a karmic component to this kind of touring, so it is best to follow your instincts rather than a map. Because of this, the wise traveler carries equipment not commonly associated with 10K fun runs. I pack American greenbacks in my socks, no coins—too noisy, plus I still haven't figured out how to use foreign pay phones. I also carry my tourist card (police are prissy about identification), a compass, and a card bearing the name and address of my hotel (you'll see why.) The little extra weight is worth it. I have jogged through cities all over the world and, not so surprisingly, the most lasting impressions I have of those cities were collected while running. In my mind, Lima, Peru, is crumbling Castillian architecture and political graffiti on the walls of alleys where children, too hopeless to make eye contact, sleep on cardboard pallets. Managua, Nicaragua, is smog and traffic, rain-slick sidewalks, and baseball fanatics eating bocas outside Mad Monk Stadium while waiting for the game to begin. Perth, Australia, is clean streets, safe parks, and black swans; Singapore is cleaner streets, even safer parks, and plenty of whack-happy rattan growing down by the river. Kota Kinabalu, Borneo, is bamboo forests on the outside of town, filthy rivers, and whole hillsides ablaze, slashed, and burned.

Anchorage, Belize, Galway, Hong Kong, Kuala Lumpur, Medan, Quito, Havana, Sydney—these aren't just sterile cities any more. They are side streets, the odors of suppers cooking, traffic, shopkeepers sweeping, a stranger's gaze from a balcony window, and other small intimacies. One of the great things about running is that there is no profit in bothering a runner. They are sweaty, walletless, and have too much momentum to mess with. On one of the few occasions that I was stopped, it was by a desperate man who didn't want money—just important information. The man taught me much about how Americans are perceived in the far corners of the earth, and it is just one example of how educational a running tour can be. This was in Nadi, on the west coast of Viti Levu, Fiji, where I had to lay over for a couple of days on my way to another destination. Nadi is not a pretty city. Because of the International Airport there, it is a jumble of duty-free shops and cheap hotels that smell of pineapple and kava. Fiji lies between the equator and the Tropic of Capricorn, so it is brutally hot; a terrible place to run at midday. But, as I said, the curse is unyielding, plus I was loony with jet lag, and jogging gave me something to do while waiting for the beer locker to open at my hotel. So I ran each day, and each time I ran, concerned strangers would stop their cars and ask polite questions before offering me rides. Why was I running in this heat? Was something chasing me?

I became accustomed to the inquiries, so was not surprised when a tiny East Indian man pulled off the road, stepped from his car and called to me, "Sir—I would be happy to drive you."

I said that I would rather run.

"Ah! You are an American, then?"

Either crazy, or an American—those were the clear options.

I said that I was an American.

The East Indian seemed delighted out of proportion to the circumstances. "Really? Is it true? An American!" Then, without even the briefest preamble, the little man hurried to my side and, while shaking my hand, said, "Thank God I've met you! I've just been married, and you will know. Please tell me—what can a man do to cure premature satisfaction?"

Yes, there are still places where people believe that Americans have an answer for everything. But my reply to this desperate man was not equal to the pride he had stirred in me: "Geezzus, that's right—you guys don't play baseball in Fiji, do you?"

Keep in mind that this kind of running is not sport. Road racing is for amateurs, and for certain situations where dogs are involved. I do not run fast, and I wouldn't even if I could—which I can't. This is explorationing in its most intimate form, with all the inherent risks implied, which is why I now carry the aforementioned equipment. To illustrate: Last year, I arrived in the Vietnamese capital of Hanoi, numbed by flight and too many stops in way too many cities. It was after dark when I got to my downtown hotel, and it was still dark when I awoke at 3 A.M. On the far side of the earth, 3 A.M. to 6 A.M. are peak jet lag hours. The brain is disoriented but the body is ready to kick names and take butt. Two hours later I was still awake, but at least the window of my hotel room was beginning to pale, so I pulled on a sweatshirt, shorts, and shoes, and went outside for my get-acquainted run. January in Hanoi is cold, and this happened to be January. It was misting rain, too. Through the gloom, streetlights showed yellow wedges of road, so I jogged from wedge to wedge. I didn't mind getting wet. Anything is better than being alone in a hotel room, wrestling with jet lag.

Gradually, over twenty minutes, the fog became radiant. Somewhere, the sun was up. I began to recognize shapes. There were trees, there were old men pushing carts, there were people by a lake doing t'ai chi, a traditional morning exercise, and there was a pagoda on the lake with a big red star affixed to it: Thus I knew I was in some kind of public park. I ran through the park, crisscrossed some narrow streets, then decided to head back to my hotel. To do that, I believed, I had to first return to the park. But I couldn't find the park. I tried to retrace my route, but all the streets looked the same. By now, the fog had lifted, but it was still raining. I had been running for forty-five minutes, so I slowed to a walk and began to take seriously the job of finding that damn park.

No luck. The thing had disappeared; evaporated with the fog. I tried to ask for directions, but no one I met spoke English, and my pantomime of trees and t'ai chi only produced nervous laughter. I spent another half hour searching, then decided enough was enough, it was time to get a cab. I didn't have any money, but the driver would certainly be willing to wait while I went to my room for cash. And that's when I had a terrible realization: I didn't know the name of my hotel. Worse, I wouldn't recognize the place if I saw it because I had arrived at night and left before first light.

It is an awful thing to be alone, lost, and penniless in a big city, especially when one is soaked to the bone, wearing nothing but running clothes. And it is humiliating to wander from hotel to hotel, asking desk clerks, "Do you recognize me? Am I staying here?" Luckily for me, I met an Australian who seemed happy to spend two hours chauffeuring me from door to door, but one should never plan on such good fortune. That's why I now always run with a card bearing the name of my hotel, personal identification, and plenty of money for refreshments. This equipage is imperative, for the curse of the Temple of the Giant Jaguar is without sympathy, and maps don't come with this terrible Mayan whammy.

SHARK FROM A KAYAK

FOR THREE DAYS I FISHED hard from my kayak; couldn't find a shark. Last night, looking for nothing but stars, I paddled out at midnight and a shark found me. A big one, too. It kept circling, nosing up to the thin fiberglass skin that separated me from the realities of saltwater. Can a 200-pound man hide in a kayak? Nope, but he can try.

I live near Sanibel Island off Florida's southwest coast. Estuaries here are a broth of single-celled plankton that glow when disturbed—a chemical interaction called bioluminescence. On the dark of the moon, with the tide just right, paddle strokes create swirling comet's tails. Fish streak away with the trajectory of meteorites. The path of every moving creature is illustrated by its own glittering contrail, which is how I knew that something big was approaching.

I was in waist-deep water when I saw a phosphorescent mass in the distance. It throbbed dull green, then bright green in serpentine rhythm. I watched it drawing closer as if vectoring toward some target, and then I realized that the target was me. Such realizations touch a primitive chord. It causes the nostrils to flare and the heart to shunt blood as the limbic brain assumes direct communication with the eager feet. Running, however, is an unsatisfactory option when a couple of miles from shore in a kayak. Not that I didn't give it some thought.

I stopped paddling. Silence is a sophisticated form of flight. Cowards and possums both think it is true. I listened to my own heartbeat, my own careful breathing as a shark, silhouetted in glittering green light, cruised slowly past. The creature was wider than my kayak, more than half as long. See a shark that large and you correctly think of it as an animal, not simply as a "fish." This animal was on the prowl. It was aware of movement, aware of life. The life was mine.

I am not a romantic when it comes to sharks, nor am I prone to panic when around them. For thirteen years, I was a saltwater fishing guide at Sanibel's Tarpon Bay Marina. For some of those years, I tagged sharks for the National Marine Fisheries Service. I've handled hundreds of the things—enough to know that they are not sinister, nor scheming, nor deceptive, nor evil. Indeed, they are complex, sensitive creatures. Hollywood is prone to exaggeration. Some shock, huh? Had my encounter been staged for the films, the shark would have torpedoed me out of the kayak, waited for the appropriate close-up, then demoted me to a very low rung on the food ladder.

Instead, the animal cruised by a final time, close enough to touch. Then it vanished into its own world, the rhythm of its caudal fin lucent and steady as a heartbeat.

WHY FISH FOR SHARKS FROM A KAYAK? I can't think of a single good reason. But isn't that one of the great things about paddling? If it offers an excuse to get out on the water, even a bad reason is good enough to justify crazed behavior. Here's why I told myself I should catch a shark while in my kayak: My old house sits on the remains of a shell pyramid that was inhabited for more than a thousand years by the indigenous people of this coast, the Calusa. The Calusa were once the region's dominant tribe. They built shell pyramids, plazas, and elaborate canals. They founded a sophisticated society that supported an elite military and exacted tribute from towns hundreds of kilometers away. The Calusa were expert hunters and fishermen—for them, catching sharks from their dugout canoes was commonplace.

I like that. I also like the fact that my two-seater kayak rests on its side at the edge of the mound, probably not far from where, for centuries, other canoes were towed to rest. I like the fact that, when I rake the black dirt in my garden, I find chunks of pottery—remnants of bowls used to feed fishermen who walked this mound centuries before me. I also enjoy the realization that, each time I take paddle in hand, there is a metaphorical linkage across ten centuries; a connection of which I am a very real part. Such things insinuate genetic memory.

After disease decimated the Calusa, Anglo subsistence farmers settled my mound and similar mounds around Florida. The shell pyramids were the only high ground in a region of water commerce. In those days, travel and fishing were done under sail or by paddle.

These days, a few of us do it, still.

LET'S GET THE HARDWARE business out of the way. Read almost any article about shark fishing and it will parrot the traditional line: Always use wire leader.

I disagree for a couple of reasons. Wire is a pain to work with. It kinks and it cuts fingers and, when using live bait, I believe it hampers a natural, finny contortionism that is nature's way of advertising. Also, I believe that using wire leader reduces the number of strikes that we may get on a given fishing day. Yes, we may catch a shark or two, but our incidental catch probably almost certainly won't include more selective, perceptive species such as (in Florida) snook, redfish, tarpon and sea trout, bonefish and permit. Another argument against wire is that, in the course of a long fight, it can slice the hell out of a shark's mouth.

Woven wire and crimped sleeves are a better choice. Particularly when fly-fishing, though I dislike woven wire as well. There is something grotesque about using a shock tippet of steel to divide a precisely tied fly leader and a delicately tied fly. Plus, in the instant of presentation, there is the ugly fulcrum effect of wire leader catapulting over mono, a jarring visual that puts one in mind of a Slinky tipped with feather.

Personally, I prefer standard monofilament leader. Buy the good quality stuff; line that is water-clear and either prestraightened or easily straightened off the coil. Won't a shark's teeth cut through mono? You bet. Occasionally, that's exactly what will happen. But lots of times (most times, in my experience) you'll hook the shark shallow enough in the mouth so that its teeth will never come in contact with the leader. Using a long-shanked hook improves your odds.

A more important consideration, I believe, is the length of your leader. It's been my experience that sharks more often cut the line with their tail rather than their teeth, so, depending on the length of the shark you hope to catch, tie your leader accordingly.

I took a couple of spinning rods. Both were Loomis graphites, one a six-and-a-half-foot medium action loaded with twelve-pound test; the other a seven-foot medium heavy action spooled with fifteen-pound test. On each, I doubled the line with a Bimini twist knot, tied on three feet of twenty-pound test running leader, and then a foot or so of sixty-pound test. That way, I could easily reel up to within a foot of my bait, which made for easy casting.

This may seem like very light tackle, indeed, but that's because I had the advantage of fishing from a kayak. Advantage? Absolutely. Unless you are casting around docks, bridges or brush, you can fish lighter tackle from a kayak because, if you hook something really big, your boat acts as a natural drag system.

That was my experience, anyway. After finally hooking a decent-sized shark, the "sleigh-ride" effect is what I came to call it.

EACH SPRING AND SUMMER on Florida's Gulf coast, several species of sharks move up onto the flats to feed. "Flats" has become a generic saltwater term to describe a topography of bottom that is only a few feet below sea level. Typically, a flat is guttered with creeks and pot holes, alive with sea grasses, corals, and sponges, and always affected by the wash of tides.

Flats are wonderful places for a paddler. If the water's clear, you can ghost-up on marine dramas that no powerboat or aquarium owner will ever see. Something else? If need be, you can always walk your boat at least most of the way home. That's how shallow they are.

A popular shark to catch on light tackle is the black tip, a widely spread tropical shark that will hit live bait, lures, and flies. Black tips are fun to catch because they hit hard, jump with regularity, plus they are pretty good to eat if cleaned quickly and properly.

The first few times I paddled out, I was hoping to catch a black tip. I had live pinfish in the bait bucket and Styrofoam bobbers under which to float them. I drifted across the flat that separates my Indian mound from the mounds on neighboring islands—a historic fishing ground.

I caught two decent-sized sea trout, which I released, but no sharks.

I anchored on a couple of ambush points that are normally productive.

A similar story: A sea trout, a small snook, but no sharks.

In South Africa and Australia, I have been in vessels (or down in a cage) while my boat mates ladled fish guts, oil, and viscera into the water, hoping to attract predators—another way that nature advertises. Yet I was reluctant to resort to chumming to bring fish around, though drifting with frozen chum or "burly" in a net sack can be a very effective way to fish.

I'm not a purest, but I do have a few murky guidelines by which I attempt to steer my life. Carrying stinking, frozen chum in my pretty kayak crosses one of those lines.

I wasn't beaten yet.

It was late in the season for black tips. So why not set my sights on another species? Only a half mile or so from my home, in less then ten feet of water, is an imploded reef of rock ledges and soft coral. One afternoon my sons, who are enthusiastic snorkel divers, returned home to tell me about all the big grouper and nurse sharks stacked there.

"Nurse sharks?" I asked.

"A bunch," my youngest son replied. "Couple of them were eight footers, easy. They just laid there, looking at us. One of them took a grouper I speared."

The nurse shark is a sluggish, docile creature found from Rhode Island to Brazil and best known for biting boneheaded SCUBA divers who think it's daring to grab and ride a "shark." True, a nurse shark's teeth are flat as those of an old dog, but they still have some power in those jaws. They've left more than one SCUBA diver bruised and without a ride.

I had a new quarry.

My home is separated from the Gulf of Mexico by dozens of mangrove islands that are neat as hedgerows, shaped by storm wind. The few islands on which the Calusa built mounds are easily identified because of the mushroom-shaped domes that rise above the mangroves. The domes are a jungle of gumbo limbo trees, tropical hardwoods, and vines. It is pleasant to paddle close enough to smell the rain forest gloom of those islands. It is pleasant to, once again, move canoe shadow around their perimeters. I would paddle and drift, drift and paddle until I was close enough to the imploded reef to cast.

It didn't take long to get a hit—a grouper. That's my guess, anyway, for the fish instantly powered itself into the rocks and was gone. Because I wasn't anchored, I couldn't stop its run. The next few casts, more grouper hit with an impact comparable to hooking a Suzuki as it zoomed passed. I did manage to land one (a grouper, I mean). It was small; couldn't have weighed more than a couple of pounds.

Then, finally, I hooked what had to be a big nurse shark.

How did I know? Because, had it been a grouper, it would have dived for the rocks. It didn't. Had it been a stingray of size, it would have screamed off a hundred yards of line with a gradual upward angle of ascent that is unmistakable. It couldn't.

No, this fish plodded away from the reef as if it didn't know it was hooked, not fast but with torque that was all the more impressive because it pulled me and my kayak right along behind. It is an unusual feeling to be towed by something beneath the surface, and kind of fun, too. But just as nurse sharks aren't known for their speed, neither are they known for their endurance. I soon had the thing on the surface, a four-footer with beautiful skin the color of buckskin leather. I held it by its tail until I was certain it was rested and revived, then pushed it on its way.

I'd caught a shark from my kayak. The shark that remained in memory, though, was the animal that found me on the dark of the moon. Like a wind that blows fresh out of Cuba, some things touch a chord.

JOURNEY INTO MIDDLE AGE

SEVERAL MONTHS AGO, a buddy of mine—a former big-time hockey player who is now an investment guru—wrestled me into a companionable headlock and whispered into my ear: "Rando. Rando! I'm really worried about something, man. My tallywhacker's shrinking. I mean it! Every time I check, it just keeps getting smaller and smaller."

Still trapped in the headlock, I said, "What? Huh? Get your hands off me!"

After years of legalized thuggery, hockey players tend to have a wonderfully twisted view of reality. Still, it was not an ideal place or time for idle chat. I was, at that moment, standing near a podium about to launch into a speech before two- to three-hundred people. Images of a friend's diminished member did not blend pleasantly with the topic of my lecture.

But my buddy would not relent. "I'm worried sick," he whispered. "I feel like one of those munchkins in a damn science-fiction flick. To take a whiz? I have to goose myself and grab the little bastard when he jumps out. My God—what the hell's happening to us?"

It is a question that, sooner or later, we all ask ourselves. From city to city, from sea to shining sea, is there a man of our generation who is unscathed by the trials of middle age? By the potential for goofball behavior that makes the worst of us look like lobotomy candidates, the rest like adolescent dumb asses?

Let us hope that we are not alone.

How about you? Are you over thirty-five? Has a physician recently stuck a tube up you? Have you become a stranger to the friend who was once your wife? Do you have a buddy who is being torn to emotional shreds because he's contemplating leaving his family for what the poor mullock believes is his "soul mate"? Do you have to make an appointment to see your own children? Have you attended the funeral of a former teammate? Do you lie sleepless at night, panicky because of financial obligations, or suffering a sweaty, nonspecific guilt? Do you awaken between 2:00 and 4:00 A.M. feeling as isolated as a small-town bus stop and spooked by the frailty of your own heartbeat?

Sound familiar? Let's keep going: When you pose sideways before a mirror, does it appear as if you were recently goosed by an air hose? Do you desperately wish there was some way to jump-start your life, to get back into shape, to slow the strangely frenetic momentum that is carrying you beyond middle age and toward some hellish existential abyss? Are you discovering that some of your old-time "buddies for life" are actually spineless underachievers and fair-weather clones? Are you bone-weary of the premise that guys like us are an evil entity, are responsible for every economic, racial, social, and gender inequity? And when confronted with that premise, have you used the words "Fumbuck," "Pat Ireland's ass!" and, "Surfers rule"?

Terrific. No, I mean it—great! If you answered yes to six or more of these questions, then you are a teammate, a brother, a dugout buddy. If you answered yes to nine or more of these questions, you may rightly consider yourself among the emotionally whacked-out elite and Team Leader of our generation. Either way you've found a home here.

No, we're not the first generation to endure middle age, but we are the largest group to enter its strange corridors, and we are healthier and more active than our predecessors. They were old. We aren't.

So why piss away this gift of time and good health by allowing ourselves to be made miserable by the common traps of this life stage? The rule here is simple: Any man who can't profit from middle age by God deserves to suffer.

Another reason I'm writing this is that I'd hate to think my buddies and I are going through this lunacy by ourselves. That's the way it feels, though: as if we were stumbling alone and bat-blind through middle age, operating without a net, all of us balding and in varying racial shades from white to black, butt-dumb in terms of why we feel the way we do, and generally embarrassed by the way we look and the way we are driven to behave.

Yep, that's right—driven.

The popular social assessment is that we are enjoying a middle-age fling or going through male menopause or that we are self-obsessed and indulging in a second childhood. They say, "Oh, he's just going through a phase."

Our reply? Bull. We resent the trivialization of a male life passage that is as inexorable as birth or death. We may be a little crazed, it's true, but my friends and I certainly haven't enjoyed what, at times, seems like the emotional roller-coaster ride from Planet Schizo. Furthermore, we resent it when the decisions we make during this, the most difficult and confusing stage of our lives, are dismissed as if we'd invested no more thought or feeling than dogs deciding whereupon to pee.

Let's examine this generalization in the cold light of reason: Broadly speaking, we are men born between the years 1940 and

1965. Most of us are late fifties expatriates who weathered Beatle-mania, moon landings, Vietnam, assassinations, and race riots; guys who exited a little scarred but more or less intact into a strange and politically correct society that is ripe with a herdlike animus toward men of our generation. Why? Who cares why? The animus exists. It's all we need to know.

What most of us are is a bunch of good-timers and ex-jocks who've found our way into various branches of the Establishment but who've never been ingested by it. Or so we would like to believe. There are some bad cattle among us, but most of us are decent people who come as close as we can to behaving the way society expects us to behave.

This is a key truth that bears repeating: We are decent guys who come as close as we possibly can to doing exactly what is expected of us.

We tend to be competent and steadfast at work. We pay our taxes and obey laws, and we are absolutely dependable in terms of our financial and ethical obligations to family, friends, and community. Some of us will run for office. Many of us drink beer. We like to work out; we care about playing the sports we love, but none of us has ever nor will we ever look like the guy on the cover of this fine magazine. Our children come first. They always, always come first. People rely on us because we are reliable. For two decades or more, most of us not only have shouldered this responsibility, we've taken pride in our commitment to the cause. Agreed?

Damn straight.

So why, during our middle years, do so many of us seriously reexamine the way we are living our lives? More important, why does this reexamination create an emotional turmoil so hellish that it rocks us to our foundations?

Middle-age fling indeed! There is nothing frivolous about what we feel or experience. Worse, no book that I've read nor any interview with a psychologist, sociologist, or researcher has come anywhere close to verbalizing the truth of our experience. That's because only we know the truth, and the truth we know is born in us, and it is a dangerous, dangerous thing to risk honesty in these politically correct times.

But what the hell, guys like us tend to be open and honest when we're off by ourselves. Who else has the balls or the wisdom? It's time someone finally nailed the head of this beast, middle age, to the floor, and we're just the guys to do it. That is, after all, our way: First kill it, then study it.

Okay, so let's begin by tossing a crumb of reality to women, academicians, and other outsiders, something we know in our heart of hearts as true: Men of our generation invest a lot of thought and emotion and angst before we decide to go ahead and screw up our lives anyway.

We are not trivial people.

Last summer I traveled to the east coast of Australia, where I rented a little beach apartment and spent two weeks alone at a place north of Brisbane called Mooloolabah. I pretended that I required distance and isolation to finish a novel. It was a lie. Actually, I went in search of a retreat; an isolated place to regroup and accomplish what I'd tried but failed to accomplish back home in the States. I wanted to reenergize my life by regaining control of my own behavior. I also wanted to reduce and define, in the simplest possible terms, the most common problems of middle age and thereby isolate (I hoped) the drive or emotion that is at the root of our turmoil.

With me I took a copy of *Silent Options,* a novel written by my friend Cmdr. Larry Simmons. I'd met Simmons years ago when he was in charge of BUDS/SEALS training at the Naval Special Warfare base in Coronado, California. I'd recently asked Larry for some SEAL-like guidance on the best way for guys our age to reassume emotional and physical command of our lives. On the inside cover of Simmons's book, I had noted three key bits of advice: (1) The body you live in is the only body you will ever have. Acknowledge that, then repeat it like a mantra while you exercise. (2) Create reachable goals, then write out a contract to reach these goals, and sign it! DO IT NOW, DUMB ASS! (3) Always work out at dinner time. And remember: No one else gives a hard shit.

So that's exactly what I did in Australia. To symbolize my commitment, I did something I'd never before found the strength to do: I quit using Copenhagen snuff after more than twenty-two years of a one-can-a-day addiction. I jogged on the beach every morning. Each afternoon, I rented a long board and let the coral sea beat the bejesus out of me as I attempted to surf.

The long board was a generational symbol that I found appropriate and pleasing. It defined what we are: social beings who are set apart; not as quick or sleek as we once were, but who are still out there seeking, anticipating . . . wise enough to know that it's dumb to waste time waiting on perfect waves.

It was at the Alex Surf Club that I wrote: "Middle age is defined by the first unexpected death of a friend and the awareness that your own life is dissipating at speed. We realize we must rush to do all the things we've left undone. We confront the final straightaway."

After a few days and some thought, I then added: "If society views our resulting behavior as adolescent then, as a group, we should invite society to the county square where it can kiss our respective asses. The point is, if a middle-aged man is not happy with his life, he has a generational obligation to change his life. As long as he is faithful to his financial and familial obligations, it's ridiculous to feel guilty for wanting to experience all that he can."

Yes, indeed, I was beginning to make headway.

The club's bar was an excellent place to do research, and it was there I made a list of kindred problems, traps, worries, and fears so commonplace that they could stand as chapters in a book: The destructive pattern of infidelity. Lies women tell men. Why successful guys screw up their lives. Weight gain, baldness, and why certain hockey players' dicks tend to shrink. When our good-time habits become addictions. Why nothing on earth or on draft is more fun than fatherhood. Why we should sucker-punch anyone dumb enough to tell us that we have to "know ourselves" before we can know anything else.

The list was actually longer than that—a lot longer—and all the topics seemed valid and honest. However, my attempts to isolate a single drive or an emotion that seemed consistently at the heart of our angst eluded me . . . or so I told myself. But that was another lie.

I knew what the cause was. We all know what the cause is. We talk about it in locker rooms and on road trips and suffer constant emotional conflict because of it.

This is the problem: The expectations of society are in direct conflict with an adult male's most powerful internal mandate: to compete in the gene pool.

Don't believe it? Go ask a mature male lion or orangutan or gorilla. You will find them living alone, on the far borders of their own societies. Like eagles, they do not flock.

No wonder we have trouble sleeping at night. As primates, we are coded to behave one way; as humans we are expected to behave another. It does not matter that we respect and love one woman above all others—a circumstance true in my own life and in the lives of many of my friends. And it does not mean that we must act upon our drives. But the conflict is there; it's hardwired; it runs deep, and goes far beyond just sex. And any conflict between expectation and instinct must necessarily result in confusion.

Indeed, considering the circumstances, guys our age are damn near paragons in terms of conscience and behavior.

As Rod Wruck, one of my surf-club buddies, put it, "It's less a right brain, left brain kind of deal, mate, than a left nut, right nut thing."

Wruck's wife, Beryl, had been killed and eaten by a crocodile. Honest. His wisdom came from pain and had to be respected.

At the urging of one of my Aussie buddies, I also added to my notebook a bunch of random observations on middle age, including: Blokes who wear rugs and drive sports cars and suck their bellies in when girls are around make us all look like blinkin' wankers and should be kicked outta the club.

Meaning that guys like us are part of a club whether we realize it or not—we are linked by the history we have lived and because we are all at odds with a similar demon: our own true nature.

If you would like to join, all you have to do is raise an honest right hand and say, "Damn straight!"

There, it's official.

Don't let us down. . . .

WHEN FEAR HITS THE HIGHWAY

———·•·———

I WAS CRUISING A DIPLOMATIC COMPOUND via rental car somewhere in Central America, sipping a refreshing beverage, when I
happened to see this hand-painted sign hanging off the balcony of
a three-story building: REPUBLICA DE NICARAGUA, AMERICA CEN-
TRAL, EMBAJADA. It was a classic tropical tableau: white clapboard
walls and a red tile roof visible through banana leaves that were still
fauceting water from a recent downpour. And there was the sign,
with a classy pyramid-shaped seal in the middle; I couldn't take my
eyes off it. I wanted that sign. Wanted it badly. I could picture the
trophy hanging from my porch in Florida. I'm a big fan of
Nicaragua (Managua's Mad Monk Stadium is one of the great places
in the world to watch baseball), plus I had knowledge that mitigated
the crime I had in mind: These embassies might soon be sold by the
very commie scum who stole money from the proletariat to pay for
their construction in the first place.

At least, that's how my thieving heart rationalized it.

So I scrambled up the outside fire escape of the Nicaraguan
Embassy, ripped the sign off the wall, hid it in the backseat of my

rented Montero, then said to the armed guards who stopped me at the gate: "Hey, you fellas mind if I park the car here for a bit, maybe take a few snapshots? Team picture—how's that sound? The uniforms, the weaponry, the whole look."

I listened to the ranking soldier yell at me in Spanish for a moment before I replied, "Andale? You mean like get the hell out of here?"

Yep, that's what he meant.

I put the Montero in gear and got my Yanqui butt out of there. I felt wild and alive and full of ginger. Afraid? Nope, not really. Which is exactly why I'd created a scene at the gate. My friends and I have dealt with weird and terrifying situations often enough to have learned a simple truth: Never, ever run. The safest means of escape is almost always through the enemy's camp.

In my twenties, I lacked the chutzpah that would have let me climb those stairs and steal that sign. In my thirties, I was too mature, too reasonable to attempt it. I'm a respectable person, right? And respectable men don't behave like demented adolescents. But now, in my forties, I have been sufficiently scarred, hardened, crazed, and numbed by this nasty bastard called middle age to be on familiar footing with irrational behavior and fear. I know that fear can be good. It can motivate, energize, and elevate. Much of what we achieve is catalyzed by fear of failure. I also know that anxiety—a different form of fear—can enervate and humiliate, even kill us if we don't recognize it for the psycho trash it really is.

Here's something you can take to the bank: Tonight, at least one of your friends will awaken in darkness and endure an inexplicable, escalating panic. Lying alone, trapped in the vacuum of his own cranium, he will battle the irrational fear that he is spinning out of control. Or he may feel as if he is being crushed by the financial obligations of the woman and children he supports. Or that he has maxed out on the job, and he's being bypassed by younger coworkers.

Or that the only thing that can account for the strangeness that has plagued him is some devastating physical malady—a brain tumor or a heart attack.

Here's another sure bet: Your friend will never tell you about it. And when it happens to you, you'll return the favor. All of us are damned reluctant to mention our trips to the abyss. Why? We're too embarrassed to do otherwise. Or too terrified.

Over the last few months, I've been polling a few old buddies, plus some of the readers on subjects from mistresses to fatherhood, from impotence to love to fear. In fact, there are just two subjects we're uncomfortable discussing: (1) how stupid we are when it comes to women, and (2) how often we feel alone, truly alone, and are scared crapless. As to the first matter, let's just admit it: We're dumb-asses and there is no explaining it. And fear? I suspect we're reluctant to discuss it because we don't realize what a common experience it is among men our age.

Fear isolates.

So let me throw open the doors here: I spend maybe 25 percent or so of my life shivering like a sled dog, scared as hell. And it's not the good kind of fear; it doesn't have the adrenaline rush that we get from, say, outraging some foreign embassy. It's the nagging, nonspecific, down-the-spine anxiety that diminishes us and threatens to cripple us. The worst time for me is 3:00 or 4:00 A.M., when I awaken to the weight of obligations or deadlines or past mistakes or personal inadequacies or worry for the well-being of my children.

I don't mind admitting this, not at all. Why? Because after discussing it with guys my age, I am convinced that nearly all middle-aged men experience some kind of unexpected psychological overload that, one way or another, produces fear. For many of us, it is a brand of fear we've never met before, a fear so potent that it can infiltrate every aspect of our lives. This phenomenon is difficult to nail down because it has many faces: depression, exhaustion, new phobias, obsessive thought patterns, "false" heart attacks, panic attacks. Almost all of us will suffer one or more of the above.

But because we don't talk about it amongst ourselves, we don't realize that almost all of us will be blindsided by these goofball lunatic feelings. The fact is, if we all suffer periods of irrational fear, then even the most frightened among us is as normal as can be.

A buddy of mine (a well-respected, highly successful guy) told me about his first panic attack—one hellish, mother dog of an experience:

"I was alone at home and I felt this weird sensation, almost like a chemical rush through my brain. It was absolutely out of the blue. I'd been under some pressure, but nothing out of the ordinary, so it made no sense. My heart was pounding. I was sweating, hyperventilating, and I thought: Christ, what is this? Then I had the terrible realization that I'd completely lost control. It was the most terrifying thing I've ever felt. I was in such a panic, I took off running. Just running down the street at night."

The panic finally subsided, but my buddy lived for months with the conviction that he was going crazy.

"I don't know how many times that overwhelming terror came back," he said. "It was always without warning—always came with a sense of chemical rush, a feeling of complete loss of control and then panic. I was so scared that I couldn't stand it any more. I finally understood why some men commit suicide. You just can't bear living with fear that intense."

My buddy should have contacted a first-rate professional. Instead, he finally broke down and confided to his seventy-something father that he was going insane and would soon have to be institutionalized; and he asked his father to help look after the family.

"I'll never forget my dad's reaction," my buddy said. "I'd lost it and I was crying, and he just smiled at me. Then he started to laugh. He said, 'You dope, you're not going crazy. You're having what we used to call a nervous breakdown. I had one, both your uncles had 'em and half the guys in my lodge had 'em.'

"We talked a lot after that, and my dad finally convinced me of two things. One: The inner voice we all grew up listening to and trusting doesn't always tell us the truth. It can give us false and irrational data. My innermost self was telling me that I was going insane. It was lying. Two: The symptoms of my panic attacks might be unpleasant as hell, but they weren't the least bit dangerous. I could take off running like a crazy man if I wanted to. But I didn't have to."

E-mail I've received from men who've suffered panic attacks or depression or obsessive thought patterns echo or imply what, apparently, is one of the important lessons of middle age: Our inner voice can lie to us. After a lifetime spent believing completely in that voice, it is a difficult truth to accept, but it is true. So when that small, familiar voice whispers that we are failures, that life is pointless, or that we are losing control, we need to recognize it for the psycho noise it really is. It is garbled data. It is irrational. It is harmless—if we know how to deal with it.

"When I stopped running from my fears," one club member wrote, "and faced them for what they are, that's when I started getting better."

Just as I did, at the embassy guard post. Right there in the enemy's camp.

THE JUSTICE LEAGUE

IF YOU'RE BEING A HORSE'S ASS, no one will tell you faster than a teammate. So listen up.

When the guy at the locker next to mine exclaimed, "This . . . is disgusting! There's a turd in my shoe," I couldn't help but feel a surge of blessed justification. First of all, he deserved it. And second, the footwear fiasco only confirmed my long-held belief that participating in sports is darned important to men our age. The guy, whom we'll call Benny, was hopping around on one foot, a size-twelve baseball spike in his hand. And he was furious. Hopping mad, you might say. "Rando, you scum! This is precisely the kind of childish stunt you'd pull. Tell the truth! Did you put this mess in my shoe?"

Why spoil the moment by answering?

Naturally, I was flattered by the accusation—particularly in light of nearby suspects who were far more experienced at locker-room justice. Immediately to my right was Bert Blyleven, the great pitcher, who, as all smart sports writers know, deserves to be in the hall of Fame. Across from me were two other baseball icons, Harmon Killebrew and Tony Oliva. Just a few lockers down was former Minnesota infielder Steve Lombardozzi. Most—maybe all—of these men were in various stages of undress, watching the guy at the locker next to mine dealing with the unhappy truth that a teammate had selected his shoe in which to deposit the dog's business.

Benny said, "This isn't funny! This is just sick!"

I'll give him credit: He was half right.

Jeez, now he was waving his grim Adidas around like a weapon. I put both arms up to shield my face as he added, "Rando, I'm warning you right now. If I find out which of you bastards put this crap in my shoe, I'll . . . I'll . . . ."

He hesitated . . . and for good reason. What could he do?

Benny was one of maybe two hundred men—most of them moneyed, middle-aged men—who'd paid several thousand dollars to play in a recent fantasy camp World Series at a spring-training complex near Fort Myers, Florida. I was one of the local senior amateur players lucky enough to catch for the Minnesota fantasy team. That meant hanging out on the field and in the locker room, listening to some of the classiest men in sports talking about what they did best: play baseball.

Harmon Killebrew? When this Hall of Famer speaks, you look at the man—six feet tall, still 200 pounds, with huge potato-farmer hands—and you automatically answer, "Yes, sir," or "No, sir." You answer that way not out of fear, but because he carries himself with a kind of genial dignity that inspires respect. He's a quiet man who resonates.

Same with Tony Oliva, only Tony's not quiet. This career .304 hitter can talk about anything from pitchers who decorated their pingas with mustard and relish, to politics, to his relatives back in Pinar del Rio, Cuba. When Oliva speaks, even the inconsequential gathers additional weight or additional humor, whichever is most appropriate.

Steve Lombardozzi, who hit over .400 for Minnesota in the '87 World Series, is as genuine and approachable as any dedicated father, which is what he happens to be. And Bert Blyleven, a future Hall of Famer (if there is any justice), is one of the funniest and most articulate men I've ever met.

Not all pro ballplayers are men of class and wit. The same is true of plumbers and attorneys, physicians, writers, and teachers. But these four greats certainly qualified. So what could our fantasy camp teammate Benny say or do to threaten men of their caliber? True, he had a loaded shoe in his hand. But did he have the cheek to use it?

Benny yelled, "One of you guys did this!"

True, so true. We four or five were the first to arrive at the clubhouse that morning, and so were the only possible suspects. But which one of us was guilty?

Oliva considered the shoe by tilting his head back as if squinting through bifocals. "Mierda?" he asked with heavy Cuban inflection. Yes indeedy, it was easily confirmed: The zapato was filled with mierda. Now Oliva spoke with the easy objectivity of the virtuous: "Why you poop in your own shoe, Benny? A shoe like that, it is a very hard thing to flush, no?"

Benny was turning red. "I didn't do it! But you guys know who did. And whoever did it is an asshole!" Then he slammed down the shoe and stomped out the door.

Once again, Benny was half right.

Here's why it's important for guys our age to participate in sports: Spend too much time alone or wrapped up in worlds of our own construction and our behavioral compasses can take a dump just as surely as the mystery pooch in the clubhouse that morning.

Friends are often much too kind and polite to yank us back onto the sane and narrow heading. Our families? Ditto.

But that's not true of teammates. Indeed, a true teammate will fight to be the first in line to chastise, punish, or humiliate a fellow teammate for even the tiniest misjudgment or lapse in conduct. Why are men such as Blyleven, Oliva, and Killebrew so widely admired and perfectly at ease in group situations? Perhaps because they've spent decades adjusting and readjusting to the behavioral mandates of their teams. Picture a servomechanism—the kind of gyro device found in missiles. The way such a device makes tiny corrections, vectoring back and forth as it arcs toward its goal, is probably a good example of how teammates keep other teammates on an acceptable track of reality.

"It's like I told my daughter when she started dating," a friend told me. "If she meets a man who doesn't have close friends, who doesn't occasionally hang out with the guys, then she should run like hell. There's no bigger red flag than a man who is not accepted by other men."

I play in an over-forty baseball league. My teammates have included everyone from internationally known entomologists to medical doctors to lawyers and CPAs to grade-school janitors. One rule always holds true: Once the entrance plane of the dugout is broken, all economic and social differences necessarily vanish. Assholes, rich or poor, are not tolerated.

In the course of my years playing in this and other leagues, I have heard certain flat truths spoken in a way that changed men's lives:

"A twelve-pack a day? That's not relaxing, buddy, that's alcoholism."

"The way you talked to your wife after the game—if I were her?—I'd have left you. Seriously."

"Know what might help? Learn to mind your own business and keep your big mouth shut."

"What you need to do is stop acting like your crap doesn't stink. Because it does, man, and so do you."

Recently, I received a personal dose of behavioral therapy when a teammate told me that a heavy work schedule was no excuse. Quit acting like an ass—call if I wasn't going to make a game.

He was absolutely right.

This is not to say that clubhouses and locker rooms are idyllic retreats for men. They possess their crazies, their problems. But something I've noticed is that when men our age attain a certain level of success, we tend to spin off into our own solitary orbits. We cut the tether, which can be good, but it can also be lonely and confusing as hell. We build our own tangent worlds and live there alone, always alone. We sometimes find depression there. Or panic attacks or alcoholism . . . or worse. And that's why we need locker rooms and teammates. They thump us with the truth, herding us back to the larger, brighter world.

Which brings us back to my fantasy-camp teammate Benny, and why, exactly, he arrived in the locker room that morning to find one of his shoes unexpectedly occupied.

The previous afternoon, a teammate had made some bone-headed blunder that lost us the game in the bottom of the last inning. Benny chose to illustrate his disappointment by throwing helmets, kicking bats, and calling his fellow teammates names. This is a grown man: late thirties, early forties. Worse, back in the clubhouse, Benny attempted to further isolate himself by flashing a thick wad of hundreds and bragging that next year maybe he'd finance his own team.

I'm not making this up. That's what he did; that's what he said.

Tony Oliva and Steve Lombardozzi heard him. Men of the caliber of Blyleven and Killebrew heard him.

And they did not say a word. Not a single word.

My take on it was simple: These were seasoned professionals; why would they lower themselves to react to the bad behavior of a fantasy-camp amateur?

Which is why, the next morning, I was surprised and pleased to witness Benny making his discovery. And why, when Benny stormed out yelling, "Whoever did this is an asshole!" I was even more delighted to hear Lombo say to Blyleven, "You going to let him call you that terrible name and get away with it, Bert?"

Not to say that it was Blyleven who actually did the nasty deed. I will not reveal who that man is.

Why? Because it's one of the rules that keeps us safe and sane, one of the reasons we should continue to rely on teams and team-mates: What is said in the locker room stays in the locker room.

But I will tell you what sports archives already confirm: Bert Blyleven is one of the great pranksters in Major League history. He is a man as well known for his brilliant hotfoots and bullpen gross-outs as for his 3,000-plus career strikeouts.

I will also admit that it was Blyleven who said, "I'm going to tell Benny to keep his big mouth shut or get out."

Bert did.

And Benny did.

JOHN D. MACDONALD

THE FIRST TIME I MET JOHN D. MACDONALD was in 1974, maybe '75, when two friends and I decided we would run a boat up the coast to Siesta Key, find the famous writer's beach residence, and introduce ourselves. That we had never been to Siesta Key and didn't know where MacDonald lived seemed an unimportant detail. Nor did it cross our minds that the man might not be home . . . or that it was terribly rude, not to mention presumptuous, to go barging in on a working writer—and by boat, no less. Have I mentioned that alcohol was involved? It was. Rum with wedges of key lime. Beer, too: Tuborg beer, a brand preferred by Travis McGee. I had not yet read MacDonald's novels, but my friends were enthusiastic mimics of their favorite literary character, and I was enthusiastic about beer. In the fresh heat of a Florida morning, beverages packed in shaved ice are a pretty sight, even motivational. I was willing to navigate fifty-miles of unfamiliar water in search of an unknown house just on the chance of encountering a stranger. It seemed like a good idea. It seemed reasonable.

But MacDonald was no stranger to my friends. They knew him well, or felt as if they did, through their relationships with Travis and Meyer and Chookie McCall, Sam Taggart and the rest. They had visited MacDonald nightly on *The Busted Flush* and aboard the *John Maynard Keynes,* and they had partied with him on the *Alabama Tiger,* along with almost everyone else who knows Florida, loves Florida, or has ever been to Florida. The published word is as public as a bus station, but reading is personal, very personal, and private. To read is to access a conduit that flows directly from one human mind to another; a conduit that fuses one small life to another. We are all born alone, and we will all die alone but, in the interim, there are books. My friends had never met Mac-Donald, but they knew him. Indeed, they were intimates.

Besides, my friends reasoned, we had a lot in common. We all lived on Florida's west coast. We loved boats, and so did MacDonald. We lived in a small hardwood house on an island. MacDonald lived on an island. Our house was on the water, so was MacDonald's. When it came right down to it, we were neighbors; neighbors united not by street signs, but by strands of beach and mangroves. It was time to pay a neighborly visit.

We left our dock at Pineland, on Pine Island, at about 10 A.M. in the calm of a sun slick day. We stopped in Boca Grande Pass and watched pods of tarpon, then we stopped at Englewood Beach and watched sunbathers. It is a pleasant thing to sit off Englewood Beach eating peanut butter and watching sunbathers. By noon we were just past Stump Pass off Lemon Bay, but most of the beer was gone, and that was progress—of sorts. By 2 P.M. we were out in the Gulf, half a mile off Siesta Key, but what had seemed like a great idea back in Pineland now seemed idiotic. Yes, we had sobered. Plus, the wind had kicked up, and nothing leaches a boater's spirit like wind. Also, Siesta Key looks small on a chart, but it seems huge when approached from the sea. There was a long rind of beach, a tree line, and through the trees there were fragments of homes, hundreds of homes, expensive places on stilts with raked lawns and boundary hedges that did not encourage familiarity. We ran in close to the beach, killed the engine and drifted—perhaps MacDonald would run out and flag us down.

He didn't.

We discussed hiking through lawns to ask directions. Nope— we were too shy for that. What we really wanted to do was go home, but we couldn't, not yet. To be able to honestly say that we couldn't find MacDonald, we had to at least look for him. Honor has its obligations.

There was a lone man in an aluminum boat anchored off the beach. We approached the man. If he didn't know where Mac-Donald lived (he wouldn't, of course) we could truthfully say that we had tried.

The man in the aluminum boat told us, "John MacDonald lives right there."

What?

The man pointed at the house behind us. "That house with the tin roof. Right there!" We had almost drifted to MacDonald's doorstep.

Now we were trapped. We could have invented reasons to turn tail and run, but self-delusion requires careful thinking, and careful thinking requires time. The man in the aluminum boat was watching us. He had helped us, and now he expected action. There were no options.

We ran our boat up onto the little beach of MacDonald's house and threw the anchor out into the backyard, an aggressive gesture that still makes me wince. As we approached the house, a handsome woman with copper tinted hair peeked her head out the door. Then MacDonald was behind her, looking bigger, broader, than his photographs. His black rimmed glasses added a no-nonsense effect that suggested this man knew how to deal with trespassers. He had every right to call the police, or to order us off his property. We were salt caked, sun bleached, and scraggly. But he didn't. Instead, he laughed—an unusual Walter Brennan sort of cackle—when we told him why we were there and where we had come from. He said, "All that way in an eighteen-foot boat?" He shook our hands and pushed the door open. "Come on in."

We spent maybe an hour with MacDonald. He showed us around his house. It seemed to amuse him that the roof leaked ("Proves it was designed by an architect.") and was very proud of his new IBM Selectric typewriter, which he demonstrated ("The day will come when I'll be able to send the ribbon cassettes to my publisher, and a computer will converted it into type.") My friends began to ask him detailed questions about his novels ("God, I'm terrible at my own trivia! I can't remember what character did what to whom.") but I do remember him saying that Travis's middle name was Dann ("Two N's.") and that he was currently at work on a novel based on an apartment complex on Casey Key (Condominium). "The one with its feet in the water. You came right past it."

When I left Siesta Key that day, I liked MacDonald a lot. He was friendly and funny and obviously very smart. But it wasn't until I began to read MacDonald's books that I understood why it was my crazy friends were willing to travel one hundred miles in a small boat just to meet the man.

IN DECEMBER OF 1986, when MacDonald died at the age of seventy, he became a statistical vehicle for the neat summarization of obituaries: In forty years as a writer he published seventy-seven books, twenty-one of them Travis McGee novels, which sold more than thirty million copies in the U.S. Thus his life was distilled.

But numbers, while fine in baseball box scores, are a poor gauge of a writer's life or his worth. That certainly is true of MacDonald, whose work has affected Florida as surely as his work was influenced by Florida. When I was asked to write this story, it was suggested that I write about the impact MacDonald's books have had on this state. It would make an interesting study, and I would like to do it, but I can't. I can't because, even if I were qualified, which I am not, it is impossible to measure the influence of books. As I said, reading is a personal and private thing. But some general observations can be made about the books themselves, so a pattern of impact can be implied.

Decades before the environmental movement became trendy, MacDonald was already providing tough, insightful exposition not only on the ecological outrages this state has suffered, but also on the self-serving political networks that endorsed the outrages. In those days, it was a startling theme: Any man or organization who would destroy 200 acres of living earth for profit wasn't above killing a few people, too. MacDonald was a shrewd observer of Florida's unique social milieu as well, particularly when it came to transplants who allowed themselves to be duped by developers or con artists. As he wrote in *The Dreadful Lemon Sky*, "On the tube the local advertising for condominiums always shows the nifty communal features, such as swimming pool, putting green, sandy beach, being enjoyed by jolly hearty folk in their very early thirties . . . . But when the condominiums are finished and peopled, and the speculator has taken his maximum slice of the tax-related profits and moved on to crud up somebody else's skyline, the inhabitants all seem to be on the fragile side of seventy, sitting in the sunlight, blinking like lizards and wondering if these are indeed the golden years . . . ."

No one has been able to slow the population growth in Florida, but MacDonald did help educate that population. He also provided a call for smarter resource management—a call as powerful as his constituency of readers—that was heard by legislators not just in this state, but around the nation.

There is no doubt that MacDonald was farsighted, but I also believe that, in the decades to come, his work will also provide invaluable historical tableaux as well. MacDonald's Florida was the Florida of the 1950s, '60s and '70s, and in just a few sentences he could nail any piney woods cow town, duplex singles retreat, Keys trailer park, mangrove shanty village, or glitzy raw sod development. Describing a central Florida county in *The Girl in the Plain Brown Wrapper,* he wrote: "Black angus. White fences. Horse breeding as a sideline. An industrial park, a couple of nice clean operations making fragments of the computer technology . . . . Lakes amid the rolling land, some natural and some created by the horrendous mating dance of bulldozer and developer. Golf clubs, retirement communities, Mid-Florida Junior college.

"No boomland this. No pageants, gator farms, Africa-lands, shell factories, orchid jungles. Solid cautious growth, based on third-and fourth-generation money and control—which in Florida is akin to a heritage going back to the fourteenth century."

Those of us who read that in the 1970s thought: Yes, that's exactly the way it is. Those who read it in 2070 will think: So that is how it was!

The popularity of MacDonald's work is not a mass market phenomenon. It is the result of a chain reaction catalyzed by a solitary writer speaking to a solitary reader, communicating in a way that went straight to the marrow. This was illustrated to me a few years ago when I was invited to speak at the annual John D. MacDonald Conference on Mystery and Detective Fiction. The conference was held at Bahia Mar, the real life marina where, at Slip F-18, the fictional McGee moored his houseboat. During a break in the proceedings, I wandered out to the docks. I had been to Bahia Mar before, but I had never taken the time to see if Slip F-18 really existed. The berth was there, along with a brass plaque commemorating McGee. But the tribute I found most interesting was the adjacent piling, on which were pinned dozens of notes and letters, all addressed to McGee, each written as if Travis and Meyer were away on some adventure and expected to return.

MacDonald breathed life into his characters, and no writer can hope to have more impact than that.

Something else the conference illustrated was that MacDonald, the progeny of 1950 pulp magazines, had helped make the mystery genre respectable. There was an impressive list of academics in attendance and, one by one, they presented scholarly papers on some bit of McGee esoterica. To me, it was a startling display. Some educators, particularly unpublished educators, are quick to dismiss genre fiction as hack work not worthy of their time. "Formula writing," some call it. But MacDonald pushed the genre's envelope. He used McGee and other characters to explore dark and quirky and sometimes hilarious corners of the human condition. He used digression—normally a taboo device—to jump up on a soap box and speak his own mind. The conduit of his own discipline, mystery writing, wasn't big enough for the things he wanted to say, so he ignored the limitations, and thereby expanded the genre. For that, all writers everywhere should be eternally grateful to the man. The academics I met at Bahia Mar were open-minded enough to understand that. And the measure of their respect for MacDonald could be gauged by the number of them who took me aside and said, "You knew the man? Tell me about him."

It would be stretching it to say I really knew MacDonald, but I did tell them about the boat trip. And about the boat trips that followed. It became an annual summer event for my crazy buddies and me. It was never planned. We never notified MacDonald in advance. We would be sitting out on the dock, hot and lazy, and one of us would note how slick the water was. Then someone else would mention that there was plenty of ice in the cooler and plenty of fuel in the skiff. An hour later, we would be anchored off Englewood Beach, munching sandwiches and watching sunbathers which, as I have already said, is a pleasant thing to do.

We made the trip to Siesta Key six, maybe seven times. It grew into a kind of production. We would set the anchor in Mac-Donald's backyard, then march up to his door and present him with a bottle of Boodles gin. Or maybe it was Plymouth gin. I can't remember for certain what brand, but it was gin, for had it been beer or rum the bottle would not have survived the long trip. We found MacDonald home all but once, and each time he greeted us with the same Walter Brennan cackle and invited us in, sometimes calling to his wife, "Dorothy? The boys from Pine Island are here again."

Afterwards, my friends and I would hitchhike out to what was then the Kansas City Royals Baseball Academy, where our buddy Gene LaMont was a coach. We would swim in the pool, play catch, or just sit around and talk in the locker room. Then, if Gene's old car was working, he would drive us back to the bridge at Siesta Key, where our boat was tied.

Twice MacDonald and his neighbor, Pulitzer Prize–winning novelist MacKinlay Kantor, invited me to their weekly writers' lunch at Merlin's Restaurant in Sarasota, and that's as close as I came to hearing MacDonald ever talk about writing. Between games (they played Liar's Poker for drinks), I remember him saying to Dick Glendinning, "I hate parties because, invariably, someone always comes up and asks, 'Why don't you try and write a serious novel?' And just as invariably, they'll tell me that they've always wanted to do a book—if they just had the time." MacDonald told Glendinning that his stock answer was, "Yes, and I've always wanted to be a brain surgeon."

Even though I heard that intimidating exchange, I would like to think that it is still to my credit that I didn't tell MacDonald that I hoped to someday write books. I remained one of the boys from Pine Island and, as a result, the few conversations and correspondence we had were relaxed and unbusinesslike. The last letter I received from MacDonald is an example. It was written on his personalized stationery, address Hotel Akumal, Cancun, Mexico (the man seemed to have a fetish for stationery), dated 23 January, 1980. The last paragraph reads: "Pretty nice down here. Our little house is about 100 yards from the beach bar, where the Bohemia and Superior are always cold. Nearest phone is 60 miles north up the jungle road. No newspapers, TV, etc. As long as the generator keeps going, this machine keeps writing."

After 1980, my friends and I never made another trip to Siesta Key, and I'm not sure why. Maybe it was because we, like all of Florida, were changing fast. Our obligations became greater, our schedules fuller, our days busier, and there was no time for loony schemes and pointless boat trips. One crazy friend became an administrative chief in his chosen field. Another became the head of a mathematics department. Gene LaMont became manager of the Chicago White Sox. And I quit my charter-fishing business and began to write novels.

Then in 1987, as we all know, the generator quit, the machine stopped writing, and John D. MacDonald died.

In the interim, though, there are his books.

POISON IVY

A PERSON WHO DOES NOT KNOW the word *fear* probably doesn't know many other words, either, and most of us who are fearless are real . . . proud? . . . yes, real proud of it. But not me; pride is for amateurs. For a professional outdoors person, fearlessness is compulsory; a way of life, you might say. Dauntless, daring, heroic, intrepid . . . un-scaredy-cat-like—these descriptions apply, and probably a lot more, too, though they are not to be found in the cheap thesaurus from which I am now copying. The job has requirements, and very few have the mental fortitude that is essential. That is not to say we are idiotic; no. Just courageous.

All this being said, I am now going to make an admission: there is something found outdoors that does frighten me. Unbelievable? Those familiar with my reputation may find it so, yet it's true. And I make this admission knowing full well that it could damage my status among other outdoor professionals who, if they could formulate the words, would be quick to criticize.

The thing that frightens me is not a reptile. Some reptiles can run as fast as a horse for short distances, which isn't quite fast enough, as I've proven more than once. Neither is it a mammal, a bird, or a marsupial . . . though marsupials, frankly, make me edgy—they could be carrying anything in those pouches, and who would ever suspect?

No, the one thing in the whole outdoors that frightens me is not an animal. It is a plant. A terrible plant; a loathsome, detestable abomination of a plant. A real sunlight-sucking flora ghoul, and if I could push a button and destroy every living one worldwide, plus all its relatives, I'd do it in a country second, those namby-pamby Greenpeacers and Friends of the Rainforest be damned. Annihilation takes work, and sometimes that work is good. I'd love to just give extinction a chance. So, each time spring rolls around, I find myself wishing such a button existed. I yearn to draw first sap.

But I never have; not once, since my first encounter with this hell scum of a plant. I was young, maybe seven or eight years old. I had wandered out into the woods. Breakfast had been eaten. I was finished with it, and so was my digestive system. I squatted in the weeds where leaves were plentiful and within easy reach. I was naive in those days. I believed that nature was good, and provided for all contingencies. I didn't realize that nature could also be the party-king of bastard jokers.

I used the leaves.

Two or three days passed. I began to feel chaffed. Then I began to feel worse. The sensation was that of having swallowed fire ants who then massed at the exit region and were trying to bite their way to freedom. Even as a youth, I had a high tolerance for pain, but this was beyond the pale. I described the symptoms to my mother, who was puzzled: "Little boys don't get hemorrhoids." Then she reconsidered. "Well . . . *you* could, I guess."

Her diagnosis was wrong. The sensation intensified and spread. By the eighth day, I was crazed by the constant, unrelenting itch; by the tenth day, I was certifiably demented. I fantasized about methods of relief. Sitting in a basin of gasoline and then lighting it seemed reasonable. My mother took it as a threat; she also took the basin. Finally, after enduring this hell for nearly two weeks, she drove me to a country doctor; an old man named Beard, who was known locally for his bad eyesight, his dull needles, and his cold hands. In the examining room, Dr. Beard stooped for close inspection. The soft whistle he gave seemed heartfelt; a sound of genuine respect and empathy. "Holy Lordy," Dr. Beard said to my mother, "this boy's got poison ivy all over his goodies."

That's the plant I despise; the one thing in the whole outdoors that I genuinely fear.

With me, it's personal.

Yeah, it's real personal.

I HAVE HAD POISON IVY TOO many times to count. On several occasions, I had it so bad that I could do nothing but lie in bed, immobile and in agony, counting the days until it dried up. It never took less than two weeks, and the description, "dried up" is used advisedly, for it is an unattractive affliction that begins with a bumpy red rash that mushrooms into seeping blisters atop more seeping blisters. It is impossible to enjoy anything when one has a bad case of poison ivy. You can't read because you can't concentrate. Television becomes meaningless; even *Gilligan's Island* is unwatchable. A pet theory of mine is that the rash affects the nervous system; it transforms the sweetest of us into crabby, irrational mutants. Experts with whom I have spoken disagree, but personal experience counts for something, and it has been my experience that an ivy sufferer shouldn't be trusted with axes or firearms. Lizzy Borden probably didn't have poison ivy, but she could have, and look what happened to her.

Experts told me a lot more about the affliction, too—I asked recently, reasoning that the only way to beat an enemy is to know him. Here are the facts we should all have at hand: the bastard poison ivy has bastard kindred in poison oak and poison sumac—which is to say they are not related to real ivy and oak at all, but are fatherless impostors. Actually, they are members of the cashew nut family, which makes no sense . . . but then, neither does the existence of these obnoxious plants.

Ivy, oak, and sumac infest the United States from the Rockies eastward; only western poison oak outrages the Pacific Coast states. Their numerous species and subspecies prefer a variety of soil conditions, and so can be found isolated, or overlapped, generally making a mess of wilderness terrain in every state but Alaska and Hawaii. All three plants are very bad news, because their roots, branches, flowers, and leaves contain an oil called urushiol (u-roo-she-all); a sap so potent that a single Coors can full of it could produce a rash on every man, woman, and child in America. Not that we would all get it. According to Dr. Jere Guin, chairman of the Department of Dermatology at the University of Arkansas Medical Center, about half the population is allergic to the oil, and another thirty-five percent will become allergic to it at some time in their lives. "Sensitivity can change during the course of a person's life," Guin, who has been studying the plants for decades, told me. "Repeated exposures can reduce the way a person reacts to it. But a person who has never had it can suddenly have a very severe reaction. Only about fifteen percent of the population seem to be immune, and they are usually people who have asthma, hay fever—that sort of thing. It has to do with the way their white blood cells react."

Yes . . . or it could have something to do with a Satanic pact.

But here's what happens to the rest of us: Within as little as five minutes after contacting the skin, urushiol slips through the outer epidermal and bonds to the skin's inner layers. The body's immune system, perhaps bored by good health, identifies the oil as an invader, and attacks it with white blood cells, which engulf the interloper scum. Within about two days, the first symptom of a very nasty little war is noticed: swelling red skin that itches like hell. Several days later, the first real casualties surface: blisters that ooze serum from ravaged cells. I used to think that the ooze spread the disease. Experts say it does not.

If you spend enough time outdoors, you will probably get it, and if you get a really bad case, as I said, expect to go slightly mad. I used to spend those hateful hours planning ways to kill all of the plants I could find. Revenge, after all, is the best way to get even— but it is also a double-edged sword when it comes to poison ivy. Once I used a shovel to destroy a mess of plants, then apparently got it again from later touching the blade of the shovel. Another time, cloaked with gloves and coveralls, I used an axe to hack down some vines, carefully washed the axe . . . then, later, was again infected, presumably from petting the dog that had accompanied me. Animals don't get it, but they can transport the urushiol oil, which probably doesn't have a longer shelf life than uranium, but seems to.

Experts agree that the best way to avoid being infected is to learn to recognize the plants, but that's not easy, either. There are two species of poison ivy, two of poison oak, but many subspecies. Worse, the plants are masters of disguise. They can stand alone, like trees, or they creep up poles or fences on hairy vines. Usually, their leaves grow three to a stalk, but those leaves may be lobed or sawtoothed, bright green or dark and furry, as small as a spoon or as big as a man's hand.

"If you go around and ask people what poison ivy or poison oak looks like, you'll get a lot of different answers," Guin told me. "That's because a lot of people, even outdoors people, don't know, but they don't want to admit it. When I first got interested in the subject, I went all over Indiana listening to people tell me where to find poison oak. Well, there is no poison oak in Indiana. When I finally realized that, I felt like an idiot. I had listened to a lot of people who didn't know what they were talking about. But a person can learn what the plants look like if they just take the time to do a little research."

Dr. William Epstein of the University of California at San Francisco has been doing original research on the subject since the 1950s, and he is one of the world's leading authorities. It was Epstein who told me that some of the most severe cases he has seen were caused by smoke from the burning plants. "I have seen cases of people who have inhaled the smoke of burning poison oak and had to be hospitalized. The interesting thing is, in our studies, we've never seen a case of a professional firefighter who's gotten it that way. It has always been the amateur volunteers, or people just standing around watching a campfire burn who are the ones who end up in intensive care units. But even that's not so bad now, because we tell physicians to treat them with IV steroids, and that usually clears it right up."

Epstein said that he occasionally gets reports of fatal cases of poison oak dermatitis. "But those claims are usually made by attorneys and, in my experience, always fallacious. There is one instance of a ranch owner who had poison oak constantly, and he was the only case I have ever seen where someone actually had skin sensitizing antibodies in his blood plasma. The man ended up with nephrosis, a kidney disease, which may have been associated with the poison oak. But that's the only case I've ever heard of."

A very unlucky man.

"Yes, he was," said Dr. Epstein. "I still have his kidney in my freezer."

According to Epstein, a good thing to do if you have been exposed to poison oak or ivy is find a stream and flush the area immediately with cold water. It helps inactivate urushiol not already bonded with the skin. Don't use hot water, don't use handy wipes, and don't scrub it—

you could spread it. If you're close to home, the best way to decontaminate yourself is to flush the area liberally with a solvent—rubbing alcohol is good, but you can use acetone, gasoline, or paint thinner, too.

"They will extract the urushiol if it's still there," Epstein explained. "But don't use a solvent until you're ready to leave the woods because it also extracts the skin's natural protection."

Vaccines against the rash are being developed, but they are not on the market yet. For people who are highly sensitive, Epstein told me about a barrier preparation called Stokogard Outdoor Cream produced by Stokhausen, a German industrial supply company. "It's not advertised as an anti–poison oak and ivy preventative," he said. "It's messy, and it smells a little like dead fish when you first put it on, but it works. People who are truly sensitive to the plants shouldn't mind one bit."

As a former fishing guide, I know the odor well: a pungent aroma that, unlike some prissy colognes, makes an honest statement about one's involvement with the outdoors. Epstein recommends it. So do I.

It was Dr. Guin who told me that one of the country's most famous poison ivy plants was found on Sanibel Island, Florida, where, coincidentally, I became intimate with that odor because it is where, for many years, I worked as a guide. "The plant was gigantic," Guin told me. "William Gillis described it in his doctorial dissertation. I know Dr. Gillis, and he's a man not easily impressed, but this plant impressed him. It had a trunk as big as a tree; extraordinarily large. I still have photos of it somewhere, and I'm glad I do because, now, the trunk's still there, but the plant's gone. Someone cut it down."

Imagine that?

It's a start . . . .

LIFE OF THE CAMP-OUT

NATURE IS NOT GARRULOUS and most campers, by nature, aren't exactly Mr. Saturday Night, either. Which is okay. There's a lot to be said for a circle of introspective faces suspended above the campfire's light. Solitude. Heavy vibes. Self-exploration while communing with the Oneness of all Sentient Beings in the circular flow of timelessness. Moody stuff like that. Which is fun, of course, but after half an hour or so, even the most devout are going to yearn for a break. Let's face it, Nature may be great, but it's not a lot of laughs.

Okay, so who in the group is going to provide the entertainment? You, that's who.

Listen up and lighten up.

Firstly, things an aspiring Ms./Mr. Saturday Night should remember:

Don't bring a harmonica. If you do, don't play it. If you do play it, understand in advance that you deserve whatever the hell happens to you.

Guitars, Jew's harps, tissue combs, bugles, and flute-o-phones—ditto.

Banjos are okay.

Shun worn-out ghost stories such as "The Man With the Golden Arm" and the one about the hook-handed murderer who escaped from the psycho ward. People don't jump at the punch line anymore and, if they do, it may be because they know more about psycho wards than they're telling. (Suggestion: Make certain these people know where your tent is—then move it.)

As topics of conversation, the following are to be avoided: God, Presidents, small wars, protein diets, the Democratic party, rap music classics, cryogenics, Greenpeace, anything having to do with sex, and cow tipping. These have been the catalyst of more than one ugly food fight.

When someone begins a sentence, "Don't you think, with all those stars out there, there have to be other life forms—" instantly leap to your feet and yell, "That barking dog is giving me orders again!" It's the best way I know to ensure a fast transition onto a more interesting topic.

Jokes are acceptable, as long as they aren't sexist, racist, elitist, gross, suggestive, or offensive to people who are politically sensitive.

Don't waste your time telling jokes.

Open abuse of mind-altering crutches, such as alcohol, should be discouraged. It is sophomoric, plus, in a group situation, people almost always expect you to share.

Okay, now you know what not to do. But what should you do to bring life to an outdoor retreat?

Riddles are good icebreakers. Here's one: While exploring the Arctic, an anthropologist finds, frozen and perfectly preserved, the nude bodies of a man and a woman. Upon seeing them, he knows immediately that they are Adam and Eve. How?

The answer has nothing to do with ribs, serpents, model numbers, burning bushes, or fruit—unless you count a certain type of orange. Also, take care that solving the riddle doesn't degenerate into some inane discussion about the source of all life.

Here's another: Referring to a visitor he recently had, one prisoner says to another, "Brothers and sisters, I have none. But that man's father was my father's son."

Who was the visitor?

Again, use the time-proven barking dog diversion if conversation turns toward prison reform.

A wise Ms./Mr. Saturday Night offers no more than two riddles (any more, and egos get involved; campers can turn surly). Besides, you should have bigger and better things planned, anyway.

That's right—if you want to guarantee your comrades a night of good, clean outdoor entertainment, you need a plan. Here's one of my favorites:

Prior to the outing, recruit an accomplice. Into a container, you and your accomplice should empty a gallon or two of N-A beer (nonalcoholic beer, but only you two can know that). That night, around the campfire, lure the others into a festive drinking game. You and your accomplice, of course, will also drink the harmless beverage, all the while chuckling privately as sober people begin acting tipsy (they will; it never fails).

It's a great gambit—especially for you, because here is what your accomplice doesn't know: Into his N-A beer, you have been sneaking shots of grain alcohol.

About midnight, you may find him wandering pathetically through the forest, talking to himself: "I'm not drunk, I know I'm not drunk. SO WHY CAN'T I FIND MY TENT?"

That's not entertaining?

Hey, lighten up a little.

GIFT OF THE GAME

When passed by Fidel Castro's motorcade west of Havana, the wake of those five unexpected black limos seemed to leach the light out of our little bus, catalyzing a momentary panic. Our Cuban guide, Rey, sat straighter in his seat, whispering, "Madre de Dios!" as Lazaro, our driver, ripped the glasses off his face and hurled them into the aisle.

Crazed, Commie behavior? Nope. Perfectly understandable considering the circumstances.

The timing was bizarre. Our Florida over-forty baseball club had just beaten the village of Vinales 11-4 (the first U.S. amateur team to win in Cuba since 1959) and we were in the process of making offerings of alcohol and tobacco to our adopted talisman, Chango, the Santeria God of War. Well, actually we were smoking cigars and sipping aged rum, but our enthusiasm bordered on reverence, which, to a kick-ass god like Chango, is plenty good enough. Spend a week in Cuba playing hardball, sweating cane liquor and orange clay, and you'll come away with an appreciation for Chango if nothing else.

Coincidentally, one of us had opened cardboard luggage in search of batting gloves but found, instead, twenty new Hooters girl

159

calendars, complete with patented viewing devices. Traffic on Cuba's interstates is sparse, so it was not unlikely that El Presidente glanced at our bus and was startled to see our driver wearing red and blue 3-D glasses, steering with one hand, holding a bikinied Miss December aloft with the other. Nor was it unlikely that Fidel suffered the subliminal impression of several gringos dancing with bottles of Aguadiente, toasting a voodoo figurine on the dashboard, a papier mâché infielder in a red Cuban uniform. In the miniseconds of passing, he may have witnessed Lazaro pull the glasses off his face, but not the mayhem that followed. Being ballplayers, we all lunged instinctively to catch the glasses. Being slightly drunk, we all missed. Rum was spilled. So was a box of cigars.

In the commotion, a voice cried, "Dear God! Not the Cohibas!" as another yelled, "Keep your hands off the floor, gentlemen, unless you want to get spiked!"

Rey, who works for the government's department of tourism, turned and made a shushing motion. "Don't you understand? That was Him. The Maximum Leader! Or maybe his brother, Raul. We never know where they are, where they will be. They own the only black Mercedes in Cuba."

Our winning pitcher watched the motorcade for a moment before observing, "Classic defensive diamond pattern. Fidel's probably in the middle car. Or it could be a ruse, and he's on point. Midafternoon, security people are at the peak of their game. Too late to be hung-over, too early to be drunk."

Having run for the U.S. Presidency in 1988 on the Rhinoceros Ticket, along with Hunter S. Thompson, Bill Lee, the former Red Sox great, probably knew what he was talking about.

Through the rear window, we all watched as one of the limos braked briefly. It was as if someone had turned to take a second look—someone in the middle car.

Lee nodded confirmation. "Rey, you think he knows we're here? Or that we won today?"

Rey had regained his composure and was handing the 3-D glasses back to Lazaro, but not the calendar. Hooters calendars possess a visual kinetic not unlike ocular Velcro, so are not easily released from view. "Fidel? Fidel knows everything that happens on this island. He is a very great man! A bunch of rum drinking gringo baseball players?" Rey opened the calendar and flipped a few pages before he began to smile. "Believe me, if El Presidente doesn't know you Yankees are here, he soon will."

WE DIDN'T GO TO CUBA expecting to win two out of three baseball games (kind of) or to see Fidel's motorcade, or to be blessed and given sacred beads by a Santeria priestess, although those things and more occurred. We went out of a pure love of manly excess although, because altruism is a favorite disguise of the truly selfish, we hunted around for a good cause until we found one. We decided to collect baseball gear for a Cuban youth league team, but not just any team . . .

The previous year, in Key West, I met Danilo Arrate Hernandez, director of Cuba's Museo Hemingway. It was Arrate who told me a surprising story. Back in the '50s, while living at Finca Vigia, in the Havana suburb of San Francisco de Paula, Ernest Hemingway founded a youth baseball team he named the Gigi Stars in honor of his son Gregory.

"One day Ernest caught local boys throwing rocks at his mango trees," Arrate told me. "When he told them they should be throwing balls instead of rocks, the boys explained they had no money for baseballs. That was true, though it was also true that the boys liked to eat mangoes."

Hemingway bought enough uniforms and equipment to outfit a team, and he sometimes drove players to games in his Cadillac convertible.

"Sadly," Arrate added, "the community of San Francisco de Paula is very poor. When Ernest died, so did his team. The Gigi Stars no longer exist, though men who played on that team still visit Finca Vigia and speak of it."

That story became an inspired excuse to pack our gear and head to the tropics: Why not collect gloves, bats, and balls, fly to Cuba, and restart Hemingway's ball club?

Members of my Roy Hobbs over-forty team liked the idea, although only four of us would ultimately make the trip. Granddaughter Mena Hemingway, a spokesperson for the family, said she liked the idea, too, and offered an official letter of introduction and congratulations, which was as close as the family could come to an endorsement. It took weeks to get a phone call through to Cuba, but I finally managed, and Arrate was so touched by the proposal that he offered us a government funded trip—the only way we could visit legally because of U.S. Treasury Department restrictions.

All trips acquire a personality of their own, but this trip gathered energy and momentum out of proportion to our expectations or limited, original vision. "We're not just discussing a destination," Bill Lee told me after I explained what we wanted to do. "I think we're tapping into a very powerful karmic dynamic. Literature, baseball, Communism, plus I hear the island distillers make an excellent rum. My fantasy has always been to get Castro out on a few slow curves, then bodysurf the Bay of Pigs. Cuba's MADE for left-handers. We've got to go. We have no choice."

As it turned out, the big southpaw was right.

I'd met Lee years before as a bullpen catcher during the short-lived Senior Professional Baseball League, and thought him interesting because he was fond of quoting nineteenth century poets and wore a Red Chinese ball cap during stretching exercises. His credentials further set him apart. Lee pitched for fourteen years in the Majors, won more than a hundred games, was involved in at least two famous brawls, and was fined by the commissioner of baseball for telling reporters that he sprinkled marijuana on his pancakes every morning to absorb exhaust fumes from his body. He was a quirky, anti-authoritarian, counterculture maverick who once described a strikeout as a "fascist" device while a groundball was the "perfect illustration of socialism" because it involves nearly every defensive player and results in a collective out. Writers came to call him The Spaceman, a nickname so widely accepted that he was featured on the cover of *Sports Illustrated* in mid-windup, wearing a space suit and a Red Sox beanie cap.

Lee and I became friends over several years and through association at a couple of old man Fantasy Camps and tournaments—sporting socials in which legitimate ballplayers such as he hung out with underachieving amateurs such as myself. He was always colorful, but, I soon learned, he drew a healthy line between the caricature he was expected to be and the articulate, observant man and adoring father he actually was. He was also an intractable baseball purest. In 1979, he rejected free agency and many hundreds of thousands of dollars out of loyalty to his new team, the Montreal Expos. When he was released from the Majors, he joined an amateur team and played for free. Now, at fifty-three, Lee still plays more than fifty games a year, resigned to feed the only drug habit he's ever acquired—baseball.

It was Lee's energized pledge to join us that transformed our original plans for Cuba and then elevated them. The guys on my Roy Hobbs team rallied to the point of obsession. Well, actually, anyone who plays in a league founded for failed athletes, and based on the fictional hero in *The Natural* is obsessed to begin with. But our goals did become loftier.

Instead of collecting gloves, balls, and bats for one youth team, they wondered aloud, why not put in a little extra effort, make a few more calls, and take enough for four teams. And what about catcher's equipment? Certainly we should take at least one complete set. And spikes—the kids would need baseball shoes.

"Know what would be nice?" one of us mused. "Have simple T-shirts made. With a team name on the front. Nothing fancy, but not cheap either. That would be an insult to the game."

Our acquisition list grew and so did our objective. If we could help a roster of young players by restarting Hemingway's team, wouldn't it be better to help a whole bunch more kids by founding a Hemingway League? But that would require a sponsor willing to donate a sizable chunk of money, and where could we find a business run by people big-hearted enough or sufficiently naive to give us a check without any expectation of a tax break or the direct benefit of improved community relations?

Hooters came immediately to mind. This chain of hugely successful sports bars was founded in Florida by quirky friends of mine who are actually from Iowa, a state not known for sharp edges or hard questions.

"What do we get out of this?" Champ Regnier and Dave Lageschulte, two Hooters executives, asked after I told them we'd need three or four thousand dollars cash.

I thought for a moment. "We'll take Hooters chicken wings with us so we can be the first to eat them in Havana. I'll get a cooler, carry them on the plane and document the whole event. We'll give you a photo for your wall."

Regnier and Lageschulte seemed very excited and wrote us a check.

Prior to boarding Cubana Air out of Nassau, we took inventory. In cardboard boxes we'd packed sixty new uniforms, eight sets of catcher's gear, three hundred baseballs, seventy-five pairs of spikes, two dozen aluminum bats, fielders gloves, batting gloves, six cartons of new hats, a crate of Hooters calendars, dozens of T-shirts and caps, plus a hundred Hooters chicken wings with bleu cheese, curly fries, and two dozen Buffalo shrimp with hot sauce on the side.

"This is like a metaphor for free enterprise and the entire American system of government," Bill said when he saw what was inside all those boxes. "Wholesale capitalism, gross excess, and exploitation of the masses. The calendars alone could cause fighting in the streets. We're not just starting a baseball league, we're ideological plague carriers. We may be the final nail in the coffin of Communism."

I said to our teammates, "Didn't I tell you this was going to be fun."

IN SPANISH, THE CUSTOMS OFFICER at José Marti International looked at the stack of boxes and said, "Your luggage smells delicious. May I take a look?"

Of course he could look. On Fidel's island, people in uniform can look at anything they want, any time they want. I knew because this was my sixth trip to Cuba in the last twenty years—not that I'm an expert. I'm not. My trips have always been lazy, inattentive gringo samplers, though one visit did include several days in Mariel Harbor.

Mariel was a dangerous place, a dangerous time, and the pissed-off attitude of the uniforms reflected the war-footing of two ideologies in conflict. While visiting five years ago, that surly Yankee-Go-Home attitude had softened noticeably, though the poverty was extraordinary—Cuba's special time in Castro-speak.

This time, though, there was not the slightest hint of animosity. Nothing at all pushy or sinister about the Cuban officials who met us upon arrival. Indeed, they seemed pleased to see Americans; kept a constant, peripheral eye on us, as if they expected us to do something surprising or amusing. We obliged by juggling baseballs and giving away small gifts, but not the chicken wings. Several officials asked for a taste, but we had promises to keep.

Outside the terminal, our guide, Reynaldo Sarenzo and driver Lazaro Peña, were waiting in the fifteen-seat Toyota that, for the next week, would serve as our rolling home. It was a nice vehicle, nearly new with air-conditioning, but its most compelling amenity was a massive cooler full of shaved ice, bottles of Cuban beer, cola, and a case of seven-year-old Havana Club rum. Once we'd taken seats, Rey, forty-three, with excellent English and a likable, smart-ass sense of humor, opened a bottle to toast us and, " . . . the greatest game in the world!" but first he dumped an ounce or more of rum directly on the floor.

"For the old and dead ones," he explained.

It was the first of many rum offerings made on that little bus.

I'd done enough reading to understand his little ceremony. The island's most widely practiced religion is Santeria, an Afro-Cuban belief similar to Haiti's voodoo in which it's common to make gifts of alcohol and tobacco to dead ancestors and deities. The religion is so widely accepted that predictions of Santeria priests, the Babalaos, are reported in Cuba's state newspapers. It has become so powerful that many believe that Santeria plays prominently in Castro's political decisions, and that he could not remain in power if not for the backing of the Babalaos.

The first chance I got, I took Rey aside and asked if he could introduce us to a Santeria shaman for luck. I wasn't being flippant or disrespectful, I was serious. The entire flight down, I'd listened to Bill rave about the quality of Cuban baseball, the understanding being that we were about to have our asses served to us on a garden variety of platters. We needed help. The simple fact that the best team does NOT always win, however, is one of the game's great charms. It also suggests to me that baseball has far more in common with alchemy than chemistry. With its strange tertiary multiples and mirrored, pyramid shapes, baseball inspirits religious considerations that nonplayers might call superstition. I figured that any blessing couldn't hurt us and might help.

Even so, Rey's response was chilly. "A Santeria person? I wouldn't even know where to find one."

The chill didn't last, though. As Lazaro drove us toward Havana, we spotted kids playing baseball in an open field. They were using a carved limb as a bat, a stone wrapped in tape for a ball. Day after day, as we toured the country, we were to witness varieties of this same scene. The absence of equipment does not make the game impossible for those who love it, and no one loves baseball like a Cuban.

"Rey, pull over!"

Despite his good English, our guide was slow to understand. Why would we want to watch children playing?

But that's exactly what we wanted to do. A familiar point of discussion among my own teammates is the fact that, in the States, it's rare to see kids playing sandlot baseball just for the fun of it. Games are either organized by adults or the fields lie empty. How can an outdoor game compete with Nintendo or computers?

At the side of the road, we sat for a minute or two before we cracked a box and selected a bat, balls, and a few new hats. The game stopped when we got off the bus; players froze as we approached. Judging from their expressions, they would have been less surprised by a visit from space creatures. The boys found their feet, though, when we lobbed a ball toward them, and then they swarmed us.

We handed out the gear without introduction or explanation, and drove away.

It became our favorite thing to do in Cuba. It gave us a Lone Ranger, who-were-those-masked-gringos feeling of pure devotion to our chosen sport. But no one was affected more deeply by that first stop than Rey and Lazaro. Both had tears in their eyes, as Rey explained, "We are men, but we also have hearts! We've never seen children happier. Clearly, you are men with hearts, too You must drink this bottle of rum to celebrate your generosity!"

Rey, forty-three, and Lazaro, thirty-two, became great favorites of ours, and not just because they performed their jobs superbly. They didn't just work for our team, they became members of our team and seemed to take real joy in keeping us happy. Perhaps Rey had nothing to do with it but, the next day, outside the Ambos Mundos, our hotel in old Havana, we encountered a middle-aged woman dressed in robes of pure white. She gave us each a strand of red and black beads, then led us to an outdoor market where we found a papier mâché baseball player that would serve very nicely as a religious fetish. The woman refused money, but rummaged through our wares until she'd selected what she desired in trade—three white Hooters T-shirts.

One of the clerks at our hotel confirmed that she was a highly respected Santeria priestess.

VISITING CUBA IS LIKE BEING HOSTED by victims of a generational marooning. Each morning we'd get on the bus, and Lazaro would have some old pirated tape playing, chosen to make us feel at home. We'd listen to Sonny & Cher or John Denver until we couldn't stand it any more and someone would yell, "Rey, turn off that shit! Don't you have anything Latin?" as we worked our way through traffic jams of Chinese bicycles and old American cars.

Havana has the look of a city that has been bombed, abandoned to the silence of its own dying, then slowly repopulated. Even along the Malecon, its famous waterfront, skeletons of rebar show through col-lapsing tenements and warehouses, while clothes flutter on lines. To the north is the sea, always inflated with gray light. A streak of indigo marks the Gulf Stream's edge—it sweeps in close to Moro Castle—where men in inner tubes fish the rim of the Stream as if fishing the bank of a river. Key West seems an impossible distance, more than a solar system away.

During our days in Havana, we roamed the streets, making friends of innkeepers, dickering badly in the market place, and handing out equipment to kids. We also tracked down Gregorio Fuentes, Hemingway's skipper and model for *The Old Man and the Sea*.

At 103, Fuentes sat comfortably in his recliner, overlooking a street that led to the harbor. He had a lighted Cohiba in his hand, a glass of rum beside him, and a smile on his face. He'd been following the Cuban national baseball championships on the radio. He still loved the game.

At sunset, we'd sit at the rooftop bar of our hotel, then head to the streets to explore. The night breeze of Havana has density and a texture unlike any city I know. Air molecules are weighted with ocean water and jasmine. They've drifted in on Gulf Stream wind swales, scented with distant islands.

It is a pleasant thing to walk as a team through Havana, listening to street bands, flirting with dancers. At one bar, Bill put on an impromptu kick-boxing demonstration that drew an appreciative crowd, and seemed to please even the man he accidentally kicked.

But the bus was our true home. As we rode from one place to the next, bus windows became our private viewing screens and we'd compete to identify what we saw as if touring a museum.

"There's a '48 Ford, lime green. Used a brush to paint it. An old Merc, maybe a '56. There's a Chevy Belair two-door; imagine what that'd be worth back home. There's a Studebaker . . . a Willys . . . an old Cadillac with the Elvis fins . . . one of those Pontiacs with the purple tail lights . . . Christ, a Hudson, and he's still using it as a taxi!"

Havana was the surprising conservator of Americana; in it were preserved artifacts that marked our country's ascendance as well as Cuba's marooning, both dated as precisely as if by a broken clock. For men in our forties and fifties, the old cars contributed to the illusion that we were legitimate ballplayers again, back on the road with authentic purpose.

"The bus gets into your blood," Bill said. "Every few months, I need a dose of it. Back when I was playing for USC, we used take the bus to a bar called the Blue Ox in Tijuana for some very serious debauchery. The girls there would do donkeys, shoot coins across the room, unbelievably sick stuff. It was superb training for the major leagues.

"Another time, playing winter ball in Caracas, I got off the bus and there was this woman who took me aside, put a hundred dollar bill on the table, and said, 'I'll give you this and the best blow job you ever had if you hit Rod Carew in the balls tomorrow when you pitch.' I don't know why she was mad at Rod, but she was. When I refused, she said, 'Then couldn't you just nick him on the cock?' I told her I was a control pitcher, but even I wouldn't attempt that."

Trading stories, ID-ing cars, drinking Cristal beer, we did the tour of Havana. On the way out of town, we ate the chicken wings beneath a sign portraying a vampirelike Uncle Sam, declaring, IM-PERIALISTAS, WE ARE NOT AFRAID OF YOU! Then we stopped and spoke with Danilo at Museo Ernest Hemingway in San Francisco de Paula and got our first look at the kids we'd come to help.

Danilo seemed oddly nervous, and surprised, too, that we'd made good on our promise to actually come to Cuba. "Go play your baseball games and come back in a few days. We will have a ceremony when we accept the equipment and sign all the necessary papers."

Sign papers?

"It's the way things must happen here," Rey explained as we headed west. "Danilo must meet with party members and members of the Department of Sports and make certain that everyone gives their approval. It is a very great thing we are doing! It must be done properly."

IN THE MOUNTAINS OF WESTERN CUBA, from the pool bar at our hotel, we could look down onto the red tile roofs and dirt streets of Vinales, the farm village where we were to play our first game. The village lay in a long valley boundaried by rain forest bluffs and copper fields striated by the track of oxen pulling plows. The local ball diamond was across the river, hidden by mangoes and a grove of coconut palms, delicate white-stemmed trees with fronds that hung as heavy as macaw feathers.

Bill was sitting beneath the thatched chickee, holding the papier mâché ballplayer we were already calling Chango. In the other hand, he held a red chili pepper. We'd stopped along the way and picked a bag full from a farmer's garden, surprised that Cuban restaurants did not offer hot sauce. He took a bite of the chili, chased it with half a beer, then used his hand as a fan, saying, "You know why Puerto Rico and Southern California produce so many pitchers? Because of all the spicy food. Lots of chili peppers and hot tamales. It puts a fire in your belly and protects your elbow from harm. You ever hear of Pancho Villa having a sore arm? Nope, he could have pitched to a hundred if he'd dodged that bullet. By the way—" he swallowed the rest of the chili and took another gulp of beer, "— does anyone here really give a shit about winning?"

No, of course we didn't care about winning. At our ages, playing the game is victory enough. Why else would we be sunning ourselves, drinking mojitos, and soaking in the pool with only an hour before game time.

He nodded. "We need to pick up at least four more players to field a team, and I've got this theory that every healthy Cuban male can play baseball, so it really doesn't matter who we pick. Plus, I kind of go by names. You know how certain guys have a baseball name and you just know they're going to be great? Like Cesar Geronimo or Bernie Carbo? Those kind of names. The manager of our hotel, guess what his name is. It's Angel Cordero. So immediately, I asked him to play. With a name like that, he's got to be a shortstop, right?"

Yes, hopefully, since there wasn't a shortstop among us. Our original plan was to take one catcher (me) and all the pitchers we could gather, and that's just what we did. From our over-forty Hobbs team, we had Stu Johnson, a left-handed pitcher/first baseman/manager. Stu sells medical supplies for a living, and has loved hardball since he was a kid growing up in Janesville, Minnesota.

Stu, Gary Terwilliger (a power-hitting postal worker), Mike Sherlin (a superb realtor-pitcher) and I have played together on the same team for nine years; have come to know each other so well that our personal flaws—inconsistent curveballs and hellacious snoring—are tolerated if not forgiven.

Matt Asen, a new addition, is a utility playing restaurateur. You've probably seen Matt. Millions have. He's the guy with the Grouch Marx hair who attends all the NBA play-off games and holds up funny signs. TV cameramen love him—almost everybody loves the guy because he is funny and brilliant and without pretense.

I wasn't surprised that Bill had recruited four players from the hotel staff instinctively and at random. He'd once told me that the reason he was able to fool hitters was because he sometimes didn't have a clue what pitch he was throwing until it left his hand—not good news for a catcher, but an illustration of his trust in intuition. However, I was surprised when I met two of the players on the bus. Maintenance man Tomás Miranda was no bigger than a garden gargoyle and looked to be in his sixties. Javier Perez, age thirty-six, was gigantic—he had to weigh 300 pounds—but why would Bill choose anyone named Perez? He'd given up his most infamous home run to Tony Perez in the seventh game of the '75 World Series, and there are people in Boston who still hate him for it.

"That was twenty-five years ago," Bill explained, "and the wound's beginning to heal."

As to Cordero, he turned out to be a superb shortstop, and Miranda, who appeared to be an old man, was unbelievable in the outfield. He could still run, throw, hit; do it all. Turned out, in his prime, he'd been one of the region's most famous players.

"A guy with a name like that," Bill said, "you can pull him off a respirator and he'll slap a single to right then steal a base for you."

VINALES STADIUM IS A HORSESHOE of pink cement and rusting fence posts that frame a field on which burlap sacks serve as bases. When our bus pulled up, there were so many people milling around, we thought our game was scheduled coincidentally on the same day as the local fair.

But no, all those people had come to see us play the Vinales Veterans, the local team. There had to be two or three hundred people, many of them schoolkids, released from class to watch what, in this rural place, was a big event. There were lots of cops and soldiers, too, which lent an officious, nervous air.

The poverty of Cuba can be gauged by many markers, and one of them is that even healthy, adult males can't afford clothes. The Vinales players wore piecemeal uniforms from several teams and many eras, but a uniform does not a player make.

They could play. They could all play. But, on that day, we played pretty well ourselves.

Terwilliger set the tone and buoyed our confidence when, in his first at bat, he hit 420-foot cannon shot over the center-field wall. Everyone in the stands stood and clapped in unison as he rounded the bases—that quick, it seemed, we had fans.

Then Bill took the mound and set the first three batters down in order, throwing mostly fastballs but also two MONSTROUS curves. If you doubt that there is a quantum talent gap between a professional ballplayer and the rest of us, it is probably because you've never caught nor hit against a major league pitcher.

Behind me, the umpire kept count of strikes and balls by using five stones as a kind of abacus—a technique I'd never seen before.

In our next at bat, we all hit and continued to hit and score runs throughout the game, while Bill dominated from the mound. We were having fun, juggling for the kids in the stands, giving away balls, and the Cubans seemed to be having a good time, too. There was only one uneasy moment: The Vinales pitcher was a big guy with good velocity, a Castro beard, and a quick temper. Frustrated by the way the game was going, he finally got a base hit and, from second base, called Bill a particularly unattractive name, *maricon*. None of us spoke much Spanish, but you can't play baseball in Florida without learning what *maricon* means.

Immediately, and very cleverly, I thought, Stu, our first baseman, retorted, "It's MISTER *maricon* to you, asshole!" and play continued.

We won 11-4, which didn't seem to be a big deal until Rey pointed out that no American amateur team had won in Cuba since Batista heard the tanks rolling into Havana. But was it fair to say that we'd won? We looked at the score book and saw that our local ringers had accounted for two runs between them. Not that it mattered. We'd have taken credit for the victory if they'd scored them all. A team's a team, plus, for old ballplayers, any excuse to have a party is good enough, but this was a great excuse, and we weren't going to allow impulsive thoughts of fairness or maturity spoil it.

We sat around the field sharing beer with the Vinales players who seemed genuinely pleased for us, including the Castro clone. During the cooldown, when we stripped off our jerseys, they immediately noticed the red and black beads we wore and pointed, nodding as if it all suddenly made sense. "Santeria. Si! Santeria!"

That gave Chango additional credence. He'd been a fun little toy, but now he'd actually contributed to our own good fortune. Or so we chose to believe.

On the bus, we placed him on the dashboard, as if upon an altar, and made many offerings of rum and tobacco. Seeing Fidel's motorcade seemed a stunning affirmation of the little god's power, and symbolic, too: Two diverse cultures, traveling in opposite directions, met in unexpected apogee, then separated at speed. As one of us said, "Hello Hooters wings, good-bye revolution."

We took the party up the mountain to our hotel.

"ONE OF THE KEYS TO PLAYING BASEBALL successfully and over time is knowing when to medicate and how much to use."

Bill told us this the next morning as we rode toward Pinar del Rio for our second game. We were all in need of medication so were eager to listen and benefit from his experience.

"Amphetamines, for instance—greenies, we called them. There's nothing worse than popping a greenie too early, then having the game rained out. You spend the entire night bouncing around, chattering like a lobotomy victim. Pathetic. It's just good, professional protocol to check with the weather channel before dropping speed.

"Anti-inflammatories are another story. When I was with Montreal, I took Napersin, Butazolidin, and Zolidin to get me through. They made me shit like a fox. I could pitch in the National League but, legally, I couldn't have run in the Kentucky Derby. Not with all that crap in me. When it comes to medicine and life, never forget that all the love in the world doesn't make up for a second of inattention."

If that last line made sense—and it seemed to, at the time—it found strange application to Capitan San Louis Stadium, the field where we were to play the next two days. We'd gotten our first look at the stadium while in Havana, watching televised baseball,

Industriales playing Pinar del Rio in the final game of the league championship. There were fifty thousand screaming fans in what appeared to be a first-rate facility.

On actual inspection, though, the place was a mess. The field was in bad shape, dugouts were disgusting with flooded toilets, and the locker rooms stunk of soiled mattresses and cockroaches. It was no place to baby a hangover.

The stadium contained an additional oddity that bordered on the bizarre: The door beside the dugout opened into a pediatric facility where new mothers sat with their shirts unbuttoned, nursing infants while women in white tended to them.

Unbelievable. Gary opened the door accidentally, hoping to find a toilet that worked, then slammed it, his eyes wide. "Holy shit! Look in there and tell me what you see."

I looked and told him.

He seemed unconvinced. "Bare breasts, right? A bunch of 'em."

"Several lovely young mothers," I replied.

"Thank God." He sighed and began to relax. "I was worried that Bill'd slipped something terrible into my breakfast beer. Mushroom juice or maybe a pill."

Capitan San Louis Stadium was home to one of the island's finest teams, Pinar del Rio, in a nation that idolizes baseball, yet its condition seemed to reflect a strange indifference or vacancy of pride that did not mesh with the gifted, passionate people we'd met.

Why? We talked about it among ourselves.

It could have had nothing to do with economics. In a country with a state-controlled workforce, it doesn't take money to cut grass, rake a field, or mop feces off the floor. The decay was not recent, it seemed elemental, like the odor of an unhappy home. In the entire stadium, the only things in top condition were outfield billboards: THE REVOLUTION LIVES IN OUR HEARTS! EXERCISE

NOT OBESITY! YOUR CHILDREN MUST ATTEND SCHOOL! EXPORT
THE REVOLUTION!

Bill's line about love and inattention seemed weirdly prescient.

The team from Pinar del Rio was unaffected by the sloppy conditions—a much better team than Vinales, with several former national
players on its roster, one of whom was Porfino Pelaez. Pelaez pitched
in eight national championships and is known as "The Man With a
Hundred Moves" because he has so many different windups. He's
legendary. I'd first heard about him years ago, in Mariel Harbor,
Cuba, during the boatlift. Now at fifty-three, he still throws in the
mid-eighties and has laser control, but people come to see his the-
atrical windup variations. In one, he double pumps, holds the ball
behind his right shoe as he squares himself to the plate, and then the
ball magically reappears a microsecond before he throws. In another,
he tosses the ball up under his left leg as he drives homeward,
catches the ball with his right hand and delivers. It was like watching a gymnast, not a ballplayer.

My first at bat, I flew out to center, fortunate to have even
touched the ball, and decided I didn't care to bat against Senior
Hundred Moves again. So I walked to the Pinar del Rio dugout and
asked if our teams could switch catchers.

Of course! They would be honored!

Catching Pelaez was one of the highlights not just of the trip,
but of my undistinguished amateur career. We never discussed signs;
didn't have to. He knew exactly what I wanted and where I wanted
it. If I set up outside, he'd drill my glove an inch or two off the black
each and every time. If I set up inside, he'd put the ball right on the
hitter's hands, or just below the knees. He had four pitches, including a big curve that rivaled Bill's.

We lost 7-2, and considered ourselves lucky that we weren't
humiliated.

Playing the next day, we WERE humiliated for five brutal innings. Every batter they sent to the plate crushed the ball. We couldn't get an out. At one point Stu, a first-rate amateur pitcher, called me to the mound and said, "I hate those aluminum bats. They're so loud, they're really hurting my ears."

In the stands were a couple hundred people and, embarrassed for us, they took up the chant, "CAN-A-DA . . . CAN-A-DA . . . CAN-A-DA," to inspire us and under the mistaken assumption that anyone who played as badly as us had to be from sled-dog country.

Down 7-0 in the sixth inning, Rey and Lazaro decided to come to our rescue. They went to the bus and returned with Chango and, more importantly, the entire cooler of iced beer and rum. Rey poured a full shot glass for Chango, saying, "You are not beaten, my friends, you're just thirsty!"

He was right. On the mound, Stu's anti-inflamatories apparently kicked in, because he found his fastball. Then we began to hit, each and every one of us. In the field where, before, we could do nothing right, we could suddenly do no wrong. If someone were to tell me that scientists have developed a supersensitized voltage meter that registers changes in baseball momentum, I would believe him. The game's galvanic shifts cannot yet be proven, but no one who plays the game doubts them. The score changed gradually: 7-2; 7-5; then we had a huge rally in the top of the last inning and it was 12-7, us.

Our fans felt a part of the winning momentum, having helped change it, and they'd continued to chant, "CAN-A-DA! . . . CAN-A-DA! . . . " until we got our first lead, which is when Matt, The Sign Guy, stood on the dugout and admitted what we would not admit before: "NO, DAMN IT! WE'RE AMERICANS! U-S-A! U-S-A!"

BEING UNSOPHISTICATED BY NATURE, and ballplayers by choice, we were unprepared for the complicated diplomacy required of us the next day at Museo Hemingway. We knew we were scheduled to deliver our boxes of equipment for the children of San Francisco de Paula. We didn't know that we were expected to be on our best behavior at a formal ceremony attended by Communist Party members and heads of the region's Department of Sport.

Danilo, a respected Hemingway scholar, had arranged the whole affair, demonstrating a faith in us that we did not deserve, but that we tried our best to justify.

The morning got off to a shaky start. We'd been up late the night before, squiring Chango around Havana, making the usual strong offerings. Some of us now felt unwell.

Worse, we'd spent the last eight days in a country that has no laundromats. Even if we had brought appropriate clothing (which we didn't) that clothing would no longer have smelled appropriate. Not that we worried about that upon our arrival at the museum. Danilo wasn't immediately available, so we decided, why waste time?, and opened all the boxes. There was so much gear that the steps of Hemingway's house looked as if a sports warehouse had exploded.

Which is when Danilo arrived. He seemed, at once, pleased but stricken. "We've not yet completed the documents," he said, and ushered us into a room where a half dozen very somber Cuban officials sat waiting. They did not seemed reassured by our appearance.

After brief speeches, we sat sweating in the silence until pens were circulated and forms signed. Finally, it was over—or so we thought.

"A toast to the children," Danilo said.

We'd been provided beverages by Rey, our perceptive guide, and we all drank.

"A toast to baseball," one of us added, "the only game worth a damn."

We drank again, and the mood began to lighten.

It turned out that one of the party officials had played on Hemingway's Gigi Stars. "When you come back next year," he told us, "the men of our village will play your team, and then we'll watch the children play." He smiled as he warned, "But you better bring a very good team!"

We drank to that, too.

Half an hour later, some of us were playing catch beneath mango trees while others of us showed party members the proper way to use 3-D glasses while viewing Hooters calendars.

"I bet Karl Marx is rolling over in his grave," the Spaceman told me. "Next time? We bodysurf the Bay of Pigs."

THE SHARKS BEYOND
CAPE TOWN

———•◦•———

OUT OF RESPECT FOR YOUR VALUABLE TIME as well as the kick-butt dive destination we are discussing, and after spending mucho rands researching this matter, let's move immediately to the summation: Drop everything you're doing, pack your mask, and catch a flight to South Africa.

No kidding: If you've made plans to dive elsewhere, cancel those plans. Weasels won't return the deposit? Worry about it later. Life is short, so may be this window of opportunity. Don't have the money? Borrow it. Bad credit? Sell your body. No matter what it takes, go to South Africa. Go. Feast upon some of the most spectacular diving, wildlife, and scenery on earth. Do not hesitate. Don't mull it over, don't wait 'til next year. Find a way to get to South Africa before it's too late.

What's the attraction? Spend a busy week there and you can experience the following: Cage diving with great white sharks; free diving with an awesome population of hammerheads, nurse sharks, bull sharks, and tiger sharks (the ocean's Big Five they are now being called). There is wreck diving, penguin diving, and seal diving. Travel north to the country's tropical coast, and there are some good coral reefs near which are massive game preserves where you can track the veldt's Big Five: lion, leopard, elephant, black rhino, and buffalo. The scenery is stunning, the people are friendly, the food is excellent, and the native wine is absolutely superb.

Why the rush? In this "Rainbow Nation" (as described by Archbishop Desmond Tutu), there are more than forty-five million souls of all races, of many tribal and ethnic allegiances. They represent all major religions, several minor religions, umpteen political parties and they speak a potentially debilitating eleven "official" languages. It is this disparate mix that is now adjusting to the new postapartheid powers and liberties. With its great natural and human resources, it is possible that South Africa may become the guiding star of the new century. It is also possible that South Africa may collapse into an existential chaos of conflicting loyalties, if not outright lunacy.

It other words, don't risk it. In further words, make your reservations now before the kak-kak really hits the fan . . . .

LIKE THE REPUBLIC OF SOUTH AFRICA itself, Cape Town invites exaggeration. If something exceeds all expectation, there is no danger of embellishment, right? My first sunset in the country, I stepped out onto a balcony of the Cape Grace Hotel and thought: I have just flown the best airline in the world to the most beautiful city in the world and I am staying at the best hotel in the world which employs some of the most beautiful women ever produced. Food? That's got to be good, too.

True, I was a little drunk—*gesuip* in Afrikaans, a very common word in this commonly used language. In fact, I'd been slightly *gesuip* ever since I'd settled into my business-class seat on South African Airlines in preparation for the fourteen-hour nonstop, Miami to Cape Town. A flight attendant handed me a menu and a wine list. Wine? Like many divers, I am an antiwine snob. Rehydration is very important in our line of sport, and I prefer to rehydrate with water or beer. The flight attendant urged me to at least try a glass.

"Our wineries are very famous you know," she said.

Nope, I didn't know. Because of years of sanctions, the products of South Africa are as unfamiliar to an American as, say, the products of Cuba or the former Soviet Union.

I tried a glass of Pinotage. Amazing! This wasn't red wine. Red wine tastes of grapes and vinegar. This beverage was wonderful. The attendant was pleased by my reaction. Next, perhaps I'd like to try a sauvignon blanc? Darn right, I told her. I was open-minded. Later, maybe I'd try one of the white wines, too.

My education on wine was under way.

Fourteen-plus hours should seem like a long flight. It didn't, not on South African Airlines. The food was superb, the service perfect, and it's difficult to believe the plane had room for luggage with all the bottles of wine their fun-loving flight attendants stashed aboard. By the end of the trip, I was swirling wine in my glass, eyeing it as I'd seen true experts do, and saying dumb things such as: "A surprisingly unaffected little vintage with hints of oak and maple musings."

What did I mean by that? Who knows. Absolute gibberish.

Yes, I was slightly *gesuip*; happily, contentedly so. The fact that I was buzzed, though, had nothing to do with my first reaction to Cape Town seen from altitude: city in a forest bowl, desert mountain above, a peninsula adrift on open ocean, a civilization far out to sea.

My two teenage sons were with me. They were scheduled to take an intensive PADI certification course, then four dives in the Indian Ocean. Like me, they departed Miami thinking of water. Like me, they were dumbstruck by the power of the land. "Unbelievable" became our own commonly used word. In Afrikaans, *pragtag* is a pleasant synonym. It described Table Mountain, a rock mesa of radiant, Arizona-bright striations. It described our suite in the Cape Grace Hotel. It described the old seafarer haunts of Victoria and Albert Waterfronts, the museums, the architecture, the sea lions in the harbor, the diversity, the energy of one of the world's most beautiful cities.

We were not prepared for South Africa, nor Cape Town, nor the sharks beyond. There was no way to prepare.

AFTER THREE DAYS ROAMING the left-handed highways and wilderness coast of Cape Hope ("Unbelievable!") we reminded ourselves that we had come to Africa to dive. When overwhelmed by a destination, I have re-tooled the itinerary of more than one trip, but we were still enthused by the prospects because of several coincidental meetings with local divers. Perhaps "coincidental" is not the right word here. Male and female, almost everyone we met in South Africa either dives or surfs or sailboards. They are a hard-living people who pound away at their fragile connection to the sea and they have a lot of fun doing it. Meeting people who dive, therefore, wasn't coincidental, it was inevitable, but it was surprising that they were so enthusiastic and quick to invite us to dive with them.

"Americans? I'll tell ya, *Oke*, it's great to have American tourists here!" They would then proceed to offer their guidance ("So you won't be running up and down like a bunch of cabbages") or invite us to a *braai* or *potjie kos* to meet like-minded souls.

In a nation of many languages, vocabularies blend. I was beginning to add words. *Oke* was a fraternal, almost affectionate term like "chap" or "friend" but with implications of solidarity: solid as an oak. *Braais* and *potjie kos* were barbecue parties.

We did a lot of partying which is where the diving options around Cape Town were commonly reviewed.

Just ten minutes from Hout Bay in Cape Town, we were told, lives a large population of Cape fur seals. Seals were fun and safe to dive with because they enjoyed interacting with people. On the other side of the mountain, near historic Simonstown, lived a large colony of jackass penguins at Boulders Beach. This was a shallow water dive, twenty-five feet max, and a great way to view these extraordinary animals. But the Cape's main dive attractions are caves (Justin's Caves got rave reviews) and wrecks.

The Cape of Good Hope (originally named the Cape of Storms) is one of the world's most dangerous water passages and there is no shortage of shipwrecks to explore or discover. But where and what to see depends on when you visit. The diving season is year-around because South Africa is subtropical, generally warm, and the Cape itself has a Mediterranean climate with dry summers but plentiful winter rainfall. The winds vary, and that, we were told, is what we had to consider. Because of southeasterly summer winds (seasons are the reverse of those in the northern hemisphere) most of the diving is done off the colder, Atlantic side of the peninsula. In winter, divers move to the other side of Table Mountain.

"There are plenty of great dives with shore entries," we were told. I called local dive shops and asked dumb, rookie questions. They were helpful and enthusiastic. ("American? You're gonna love South Africa, mate!") They had a no-worries, can-do attitude best portrayed by a common reply to most inquiries: "We can organize that for you. Rest easy, we can organize it."

Undoubtedly.

Someone else I called was J. P. Botha of African Shark Diving Adventures. Botha was knowledgeable and articulate, a thoroughly impressive guy. "I can organize a dive for you that you'll never forget," he told me.

In the end, I took Botha at his word. My sons and I crossed the peninsula. We went looking for great white sharks.

WE WERE IN A TWENTY-SIX-FOOT BOAT anchored in heavy seas. The Indian Ocean is 5,000 miles of uninterrupted plain. Waves do not move horizontally, only the disturbance that creates them does—a little known fact. Like fog in a breeze, water illustrates energy. On this cold morning, the Indian Ocean was a rolling illustrator of global dynamics: wind, water, thermoclines, tidal current, mass.

There were sharks, too—different manifestations of the same energy. Lots of Great Whites. They were big, heavy-bodied animals with black eyes the size of baseballs.

I was wearing a borrowed wet suit. It was made of an amphibious green neoprene, the only one around big enough to fit me. As a result, I looked not unlike a bald man who'd been partially swallowed by a bullfrog—an exotic entrée, indeed.

A homemade wire cage was lashed to the stern of the boat, everything bucking in the waves. I was trying to build up enough courage to slip over the side, into the cage. It was cold; I was shaking. I would have been shaking even if it wasn't cold. It was then that my oldest son touched my arm, looked me in the eye, and said, "Dad? You don't have to do this."

It was a great moment, man-to-man, no bullcrap; a moment of pure concern. Both of my sons knew what I knew: If I fell from the cage while getting in or out, I would be eaten. If the cage broke away from the boat and sank, I would probably drown. My son was telling me that I could back out now and that he and his brother would think no less of me. Cowardice isn't a deal-breaker among men so close. His question described cool rationality: Was it really worth the risk?

Within the hour, I would know the answer to that. Now, months later, the answer has not changed.

We'd left Cape Town the day before, crossing Table Mountain by car (risky in itself because of South Africa's many crazed drivers) to the coastal village of Gans Bay (pronounced HANSbay and some-times spelled Gansbaai). Gans Bay, population 15,000, is a town of neat brick houses painted colonial colors: British green or white with red awnings. For generations, townsfolk made their living fishing or sealing until a few moneyed, hard-core divers began to come to see what the locals had always taken for granted: Great white sharks.

Seven miles off Gans Bay is Geyser Rock, a barren plateau of stone that is home to an estimated 50,000 Cape fur seals. A thou-sand meters or so away, and providing thin respite from the wind, is Dyer Island. The seals must leave Geyser Rock to feed or cool themselves. The water is fairly clear and shallow, and the islands cre-ate a natural funnel if something beneath the surface wanted to herd and feed upon the seals.

Something does.

The narrow water space between these two islands contains the largest, most consistent population of great white sharks on earth. No other place comes close. No other place on earth pretends to come close.

On the phone, I'd asked J. P. Botha, "What are the chances of us seeing a great white? Seriously."

First-rate watermen are prone to understatement.

"Chances are pretty good, I'd say," he told me. "Yeah, Oke, pretty good, but you never want to count on it."

Botha is a first-rate waterman.

WE MET BOTHA'S BOAT CAPTAIN, Andre Hartman, at the village launch ramp. Hartman is lean, bearded; a blue ocean veteran who rolls his own cigarettes and walks barefooted into pubs. Hartman's interest in white sharks is long-standing: As one of South Africa's best known free divers, he'd been attacked by a great white years ago and escaped by hiding in a kelp bed. The animal hunted him all the way back to the beach.

"I never thought I'd get back in the water again," he told me. "Now I dive with them for a living and I love the things. To me, a white shark is bloody gorgeous."

Hartman is not the only one who thinks so. "Sharking" has become an important business in Gans Bay. No wonder. The average income in South Africa is the equivalent of $250 a week. Shark guides charge between $100 and $170 per client for a dive. The chance for locals to make a month's pay in a day or two has created a highly competitive market plus lots of angry, territorial feelings as well. If you go to Gans Bay, you need to be warned in advance: Neither training nor licensing are currently required. There are no mandates about safety regarding procedures or equipment. Any goof can float a leaky boat, piece together a cage, pretend to be an expert, and sell shark trips.

There's a further complication: Village charter operators seem to despise one another, so they are unreliable sources of information. While Hartman never said a critical word about anyone, the other operators with whom I spoke were vicious in their attacks, with most of the vitriol reserved for an outfit that calls itself The White Shark Research Institute (WSRI). WSRI is a Gans Bay tourist operation that, some complain, dupes divers by claiming to do actual research. Their most hideous gambit, I was told, was tagging the same sharks over and over.

An American shark biologist (first name, Mark), was working with J. P. Botha and Hartman while I was there. He had nothing but contempt for WSRI. His credibility, though, is suspect. This same biologist later stole my laptop computer, was caught and run out of town because of it. ("We don't tolerate thieves and pathological liars," Botha later told me. "Mark got slapped around pretty good when the guys found your computer hidden in his stuff.")

Weird but true. South Africans are a tough, no-nonsense people.

So who should you trust? No one. Trust yourself. Only yourself. Talk to captains, take note of safety equipment, consider the vessel carefully because the seas off Gans Bay can be gigantic. If it doesn't feel safe and the conditions aren't right? Don't go. Find another boat or wait for the wind to lay down.

I felt comfortable with Hartman's heavy, catamaran hull and twin Yamaha outboards. Good thing, too, because seas were a towering twelve to fifteen feet, yet we had to endure it only twenty minutes or so before gaining the lee of Dyer Island.

It was cold. The boat was bucking, lifting, crashing. Off the stern, the cage was doing the same. The wind blew molecules of bird guano and putrid seal flesh and blood off the islands. The filth touched the inside of our noses. Seals and terns screamed an octave higher than the wind. In the water were drifting puddles of seal oil, dozens of pools, each representing the place were a white shark had made a recent kill.

It was then that my son reassured me that I didn't have to get into the cage.

He was wrong. I did have to get into the cage. I knew I'd never get a chance like this again in my life.

The first shark materialized within minutes: two black vacancies in the green murk; strange voids not instantly identified by my brain. The voids were horizontal, consistently spaced, swinging slowly back and forth, growing larger, vectoring.

Strange. What trick of light was this?

Then the black holes were skewered by a conical nose, beneath which was a grinning apparition. It was a fixed, fanatical grin, as meaningless as the grill of a car, yet it lent an impression of all that is mindless and unsympathetic and inevitable. A million years of energy were distilled right there in front of me: wind, water, light, current. It was a great white shark. It was the first I had ever seen. I have not been the same man since.

The animal drifted toward me, banked slightly, black eye three feet from my face, and passed without interest or expression. The animal knew all there was to know about me. I was a seal on a rock. Maybe I would leave the rock. Maybe I wouldn't. It was an indifferent process. A novelist from Florida? Such a thing did not exist. Water, light, tide: all else was delusion. I was wind in the void. I didn't matter. I would never ever matter. It made no difference what I was, what I had accomplished, whom I loved. My fast heart had a silly, finite number of beats remaining. There were always other seals.

If you want your every illusion reduced to the most basic elements of existence, go down into a cage with a great white shark. The question has nothing to do with courage. The question is: Do you really want to know the truth? Think about it. Think about it carefully. My son was right: You don't have to go.

I did. It sticks with me. It changes me daily.

We saw fourteen different animals in less than three hours that morning. When the largest of the great white sharks appeared—an eighteen-foot female that we measured many times—all the lesser fish vanished and did not return.

Once, as she glided close by, I touched my fingers to her dorsal. She did not respond. I possessed the weight of nothingness . . . .

WHEN WE LEFT GANS BAY I knew that no future dive experience could equal that morning with the sharks, and I was right, but we still had a lot of diving to do, a lot of Africa to see. We also had lots and lots of driving ahead of us, for we were bound up the eastern coast to Sodwana Bay National Park, more than thirteen hundred miles.

I should stop here to pass along some advice. I described South African drivers as crazy? That's unfair and inaccurate. South African drivers are far worse than crazy. They are reckless, unpredictable, perhaps fired by a wild conviction that there really is life after death. Not all the drivers. No. But many. Way too many. And while the roads are often very good, there were mountainous stretches on our journey in which the roads were worse than bad, they were downright lethal. So my advice is this: Choose carefully the sections of Africa that you want to see by car. When possible, fly from destination to destination and use a rental to venture out. Unless you are a hard-core veteran of Third World travel, South Africa's highways (and pockets of existential, roadside poverty) are a dangerous introduction to what can be a very dangerous business.

A section of South Africa that we should not have driven was from East London to just south of Durban—a nightmarish 300 miles that crossed the Transkei, a region of bad roads, tribal warfare, and lots of carjackings. Because I failed to properly research my route, I put the well-being of my sons at risk, and I still cringe at the thought of those long, tense hours on the road. I had white sharks with me, however. Their attitude dominated my own. Had desperate men attempted to stop our Audi station wagon, they would have had only themselves to blame.

A section of South Africa that I'm very glad we drove was what locals call the Garden Route, 160 miles of truly spectacular coastal scenery, Mossel Bay to Jeffrey's Bay. It is California's Big Sur but much, much bigger, more exotic. At Plettenberg Bay, we stopped at the Fish Eagle Creek Pub and were immediately befriended by the pub's owners and clients. These people were representative of South Africa's outgoing, bear-hug attitude toward American tourists. I liked sauces? Well, then, I HAD to try the local monkey gland sauce (relax—monkeys aren't used in its making). And if I liked good beef then I HAD to try the locally raised prime. Beer? Same thing—South Africa had excellent beer (true).

For an evening, they made us a part of their small family. By firelight, we watched a televised rugby game, South Africa against Ireland. Rugby, like wine and diving, is taken seriously, and we were clapping and banging tables right along with everyone else when South Africa won.

Like separated water molecules, water people tend to attract, and South Africa is a nation of water people. Jeffrey's Bay, one of the most famous surf breaks in the world, is another good example. If you've seen the classic film, *Endless Summer,* you've seen this village on the sea. It is Carmel without snobbery, a stunning place of light and water and houses built on jungled bluffs. My sons and I arrived at Jeffrey's Bay on a Sunday morning. Most the shops were closed, so we stood on the beach and watched the surfers. I noticed an attractive woman, early forties, on the sidewalk. Who better than an attractive woman to ask questions about the area? Her name was Cheron Habib. We chatted; she invited us to her home—a magnificent garden place overlooking the sea. We had drinks and were offered lunch. I would learn later that, twenty-some years before, Habib had founded her own surf clothing business and was now the region's largest employer and wealthiest citizen. Not only that, she is a major promoter of international surfing. It was this person who had opened her home to American strangers.

"Around here, water's our only recreation," she told us. "The surf, the diving." Her tone asked: What else could you need?

THERE IS SPECTACULAR SHARK diving off Durban and Protea Banks.

In winter, copper sharks can be seen spinning out of the water as you boat to the dive site, and there are hundreds of ragged tooth sharks (gray nurse sharks called "Raggies" by the South Africans). In the summer months, tiger sharks and Zambezi (bull sharks) are prolific. The best of it, though, is Aliwal Shoal. Our dive master there, Mark Addison, led us to some superb reefs and wrecks.

In South Africa, if you plan it right, you fall into an interesting pattern: dive, eat, drive, eat, drink wine, sleep, dive, eat.

Food was consistently good, and I've already told you about the wine.

Further north, just over the border into Mozambique, may be the best place in the world to see Zambezi River sharks (bull sharks), the strange animal that swims deep into the freshwater interior, such as Lake Nicaragua. Between November and March, it's a wonderful place to see whale sharks as well—or so Simon Robinson, another South African SCUBA instructor told me. We met Robinson and a dozen or so of his friends at a gas station. Yep, at a gas station. They were in vans, headed up the coast on a dive safari.

"It's pretty rustic, Mozambique is," Robinson told me as the two of us stood fueling our respective vehicles. We'd just met. Empty gas tanks are reason enough to exchange itineraries, right? Robinson said, "We camp on beaches in Mozie. We build a fire, eat the local food, drink the local beer. It's pretty nice. Why don't you fellas come along and follow us up there? We'll spend three, maybe four days, depending how the viz is."

It was tempting. What were the chances that we would meet divers who were as generous and knowledgeable?

As it turned out, chances were darn good. At Sodwana Bay Lodge, Sodwana Bay National Park, fifty miles south of the Mozambique boarder, the entire staff took us under wing. After a couple of days getting to know each other, Richard Scott, owner of the excellent restaurant, surprised us with a *potjie kos* and invited some of the local Zulus to the cookout. The Zulus were a fun, articulate bunch. We could hear the village drums long after our own party had ended. Michael Mhlanga, twenty-four, nephew of the district Zulu chief, became a buddy of ours and self-appointed instructor on his family culture. He added Zulu words to my growing vocabulary. The comfortable thatched-roofed sleeping cabanas were *indlus*. Sons: *indodanas*. Witchdoctor: *umthankazi*. Shark: *ushaka*.

At night, we sat on porches of raw wood looking through the African sky, deep into outer space. Every morning, dive master Martin Van Der trucked us down to the beach to dive. The reefs of Sodwana are described by their distance from shore (Two-Mile Reef, Five-Mile Reef, Seven-Mile Reef, Nine-Mile Reef). The common corals are prolific, the fish life interesting, and Nine-Mile is a good place to dive with dolphins or whale sharks, though we saw none on our trip. What my sons enjoyed most was searching the bottom for sharks' teeth—they were everywhere. What I found most exciting was launching our inflatable in heavy surf, and the intentional crash beach landings upon our return. Our boat driver would yell, "Hold tight!" as he'd aim the bow shoreward and career us far up onto the sand at twenty knots.

An hour's drive from Sodwana is Phinda Private Game Preserve, a five-star facility. At Phinda, our guide was Dumi Mpanza, our tracker, Alson Matthenjaw.

Yes, you need a tracker. You also could quite possibly need the loaded Holland & Holland .375 rifle that the guide carries because the animals you seek are not pets, they are not domesticated, and when you venture out into the bush, you enter the veldt's food chain. You do not enter it on the highest of rungs. Each dawn, Dumi would bundle us into a topless Land Rover and four-wheel us through portions of Phinda's 40,000 acres of savanna and wetland and forest. We tracked a pride of lions on the hunt. We found them.

The eyes of the largest male blazed at us through dead grass. Like an animal I had seen earlier in the trip, he perceived everything. *Ushaka.*

We found giraffe and rhinos, crocs and elephants and cheetahs.

We had the sea—*ulwawble,* in Zulu. We had the jungle. I was with my *indodanas,* my dear sons. It was the best place in the world. . . .

ABOUT THE AUTHOR

RANDY WAYNE WHITE, a former fly-fishing guide, is the creator of *The New York Times* bestseller Doc Ford thriller/suspense series. His "Out There" column ran for many years in *Outside* magazine. Other nonfiction collections are *The Sharks of Lake Nicaragua, Batfishing in the Rainforest,* and *Last Flight Out.* His novel *Sanibel Flats* was chosen as one of the 100 Best Mysteries of the 20th Century by the International Independent Booksellers Association. White is the winner of the Conch Republic Prize for Literature and the John D. MacDonald Award for Excellence in Florida Fiction. He also wrote and narrated the PBS documentary, "Gift of the Game," which won the 2002 Woods Hole Film Festival. He lives on Pine Island, Florida.

PRAISE FOR RANDY WAYNE WHITE

"What Mr. White is good at is finding the unbeaten path to nowhere and teaching the reader how to follow his example. . . . And what he is very good at is evoking the scene once he gets there."
—*The New York Times*

"White's exuberance and his agility with language make his stories stunningly vivid. . . . For armchair traveler and rugged adventurer alike . . . good, funny, invigorating stuff."
—*Chicago Tribune*

"A gentle humorist, Mr. White holds his own as a fine narrative writer."
—*The Wall Street Journal*

"Randy White is not simply a wonderful writer; he is a fishing guide of genius."
—Paul Theroux

"[Randy White] writes about his travels with subtle grace and laugh-out-loud humor."
—Tim Cahill

"Wonderful, hilarious, eye-opening . . . travel writing at its very best"
—Jon Krakauer

"Not just an amusing collection of prose, but also a useful travel guide. Provided of course that you don't mind risking your life every so often."
—*The New York Times* on *Batfishing in the Rainforest*

ALSO BY RANDY WAYNE WHITE
AVAILABLE FROM THE LYONS PRESS

Last Flight Out
True Tales of Adventure, Travel, and Fishing
1-59228-334-9

An icon of the new breed of thick-skinned, high-endurance travelers, Randy White is the real deal, a "mover" who has no time for laggards. Join him and revel in the unique and comical situations of each of his exotic trips. White leaves the reader mesmerized by the potential of undiscovered places and the promise of endless adventure in unfamiliar territory.

Batfishing in the Rainforest
Strange Tales of Travel and Fishing
ISBN 1-55821-679-0

Whether it's "This Dog Is Legend," in which he tells of Gator, his cinder-block-retrieving Chesapeake Bay retriever, or "Coming to America," about the stirring—and sometimes terrifying—Mariel boat lift, White never fails to engross us in a life of sun, boats, work, and sport.

The Sharks of Lake Nicaragua
True Tales of Adventure, Travel, and Fishing
ISBN 1-58574-175-2

White studies anti-terrorist driving techniques, dives for golf balls in an alligator-infested pond at a country club, hunts his fellow man with a paint gun, ice-fishes for walleye with X-ray-stunned night-crawlers, and goes pig-shooting with Dr. Pavlov. With self-effacing optimism, White captures the joys and fears of wandering the earth with an eclectic cast of weird fellow-travelers.

The Fishing Guide's Guide to Tropical Cooking
ISBN 1-59228-074-9
White demonstrates with typical élan his expertise with a wide assortment of delicious tropical recipes suitable for camp, backyard grill, or a fully equipped kitchen. From the Caribbean to Africa to South and Central America, to Southeast Asia and the Pacific, White explores it all, with enthusiasm, wit, and hard-won wisdom, in this unusual and fascinating cook book travelogue.